SON AND SAVIOUR

SON AND SAVIOUR

The Divinity of Jesus Christ in the Scriptures

A SYMPOSIUM BY

A. Gelin P.S.S., J. Schmitt, Pierre Benoit, O.P.,
M.E. Boismard, O.P., and Donatien Mollat, S.J.

EDITED BY A. GELIN P.S.S.

Fully Revised Edition

HELICON PRESS
BALTIMORE AND DUBLIN

Nihil obstat: Robertus Canonicus Meagher, S.T.D.
Censor Deputatus
Imprimatur: L. Adamson, *Vic. Gen.*
Liverpolii die *VII*a Augusti, 1962.

The articles which make up this book originally appeared in *Lumière et Vie,* the quarterly publication of the Dominican fathers at Lyons, under the title 'Jésus, le Fils de Dieu', in April, 1953 and were translated into English by Anthony Wheaton.

Translation first published 1960
Fully revised, new edition, 1962
Reprinted, 1965 and 1967

Translator's note
Quotations from Scripture are normally given in the *Revised Standard Version.* Occasionally they are translated from the French.

MADE IN GREAT BRITAIN

CONTENTS

IV

THE DIVINITY OF CHRIST IN SAINT PAUL

V

THE DIVINITY OF CHRIST IN SAINT JOHN

Introduction.

A. Gelin, P.S.S

Introduction

A. Gelin, P.S.S.

To HUMAN REASON it is foolish to suppose that a man who lived like other men, who ate, drank and moved among them, who was able to suffer fatigue, experience emotion, weep, and even die on a cross, could at the same time be the Son of God, equal to him, eternal like him, creator of the world with him. For this is to imply some sort of plurality in God: whereas the reasoning of philosophers had gradually come to realize, and the divine revelation given to Israel had proclaimed, that God was one. But more than that, to do so would be to see in a being of flesh and blood the God who made the world. Paul, writing to the Corinthians, puts it in a nutshell: 'a stumbling block to Jews and folly to Gentiles.'

And yet this fact is precisely the centre of our faith. With the apostles, we confess what they confessed, and on their testimony. The question therefore must be asked: what could be the origin of a belief in such evident 'folly'? What influence did Jesus exert over these men that enabled them one day to proclaim this 'stumbling block' to the world? Certainly the idea of divinization was not strange to Corinth —the emperors had been raised to the rank of gods. Pagan mythology was full of the loves of the gods and their offspring. But an intelligent Greek knew what such tales were worth.

Moreover, our story was centred in the Jewish world, the men who proclaimed it were Jews; and of all the ancient peoples they were the most fiercely monotheist. In the course of their history they had undoubtedly been attracted by

ix

strange gods and alien myths, but their religion was gradually purified of such contaminations and was so deeply imbued with the belief in a single God that any alien element was rejected. Their belief did not derive from philosophical speculation, for metaphysics had no place in Palestine and Plato's influence had not as yet extended so far. This God impressed himself upon their faith first and foremost as a religious value, and a religious value which was revealed. His name was not 'thought of thought' nor 'first unmoved Mover'. His name was Jahweh, 'the one who exists', the one who gives existence to all that is. He was a personal and moral God, a God who made a covenant with his people, prescribed for them his Law, demanded that they should imitate him. His worship did not include a single image, nor even any symbolic representation. His name was so holy that it ceased to be pronounced and was expressed only in periphrases. And any claim to divine dignity, to *the name,* could only be a blasphemy punishable by death.

This is the mysterious fact—that in such an atmosphere a man should appear who very gradually made a claim to be God. This man grouped around him a number of others who remained united after his death and resurrection, and sacrificed their lives for their new faith. How did this come about? How could these disciples come to believe in the mystery? how did they express it? how did they preserve Hebrew monotheism, and yet proclaim the godhead of their Lord? These questions have a vital contemporary significance for us.

Thanks to the writings of the New Testament, we are able to read an outline of the disciples' spiritual odyssey, of the development of their faith. These books are undoubtedly of late composition: Paul, the first to write, did not begin his literary activity until more than twenty years after the events. But the careful research of modern scholars has enabled a partial reconstruction of the prehistory of these texts to be made. Traces of the most primitive catechesis can be found in the first discourses in the Acts of the Apostles, in certain credal formulas. In the gospels, we have the oldest memories of our Lord's teaching and miracles. It is thus possible in a certain sense to relive the faith of the first Christian communities, to hear again the teaching given there, their description of the life of Christ, which was repeated over and over again a thousand times before being fixed in writing.

Clearly not everything has been preserved; only what appeared essential has remained. Thus it is that apart from a few hints in the infancy narratives, we have no information about the first thirty years of the Lord's life; the story begins with his baptism and the appearance of the disciples. Of the men who associated themselves with Jesus, twelve were chosen to form the college of apostles. They saw Christ's deeds, they heard his teaching, they knew him risen from the dead. And their personal experience, guided by the Holy Spirit, has been the foundation of the Church's faith for two thousand years.

Why did they follow him? They had come under his influence, they were somehow held captive, for here was a Master, a Rabbi, who spoke of God in a way they had never before heard him spoken of. As time went on they saw the work he did, they heard the words he spoke. Their expectation of the Messiah was a living thing, as it was for all Israel; and in this Jesus whom they followed they came to see the Messiah.

They lived then in the expectation of the messianic kingdom; they awaited its inauguration; in very human fashion they hoped to reserve for themselves the highest positions. Like their contemporaries, they were awaiting a Messiah who would be the son of David restored to the throne of his ancestors, who would inaugurate a new epoch by liberating his people. But Jesus' references to the mysterious figure of the Suffering Servant of Isaiah, and his references to his own sufferings, occasionally disturbed their dreams, leading them to suspect that there was to be a different consummation to their hope. They were even more disconcerted by the strange title 'Son of Man', from Daniel and some of the other Apocalyptic writings, which Jesus applied to himself.

As far as the apostles were concerned there was, therefore, a definite obscurity about the personality of their Master. They had the vague, uneasy awareness that there was something in Jesus that went beyond the ordinary run of human nature.

'No man has ever spoken like this one'
'What sort of a man is this?'

Moreover, he forgave sins and treated the Sabbath and the Law as his own; and these were divine prerogatives. There was evident in this being of flesh and blood such assurance, such power and majesty that the disciples were aware of being in the presence of a living mystery. He often let them catch a slight hint of his unique relationship with Jahweh, of his glory even. An aura of the divine presence surrounded him.

But Jesus did not reveal his true nature to them in a flash; his method of teaching was a slow one. Progress was always at the rate proportionate to their understanding, with the complete revelation kept for much later, because he must undergo that moment of scandal, the death upon the cross. At that moment they all deserted him, Peter denied him, and only John was found present at the hour of darkness.

It was the Resurrection and the apparitions of Christ which opened the eyes of the disciples to their Master's exaltation and glory. His divine stature became known to them in this paschal experience. The coming of the Spirit reminded them of the teaching they had received, so that they understood anew the words they had heard and the miracles they had seen. The Law and the Prophets, which Jesus had so often invoked, became clear and rich in presentiments. A complete upheaval of their religious ideas had then to take place : to admit that God had a Son, who was this Jesus; that the Jesus they had known as a man was God himself 'by whom all things were made'. They no longer saw him simply as the Master or Messiah but as the Word itself, the power of God. No act of faith has ever been greater than theirs. It is almost impossible for us Christians, brought up in the Christian faith, to measure its depth, for it was the complete reversal of a religious attitude, as total as that experienced by Paul on the Damascus road.

The faith which the apostles received as a living seed had to find a vocabulary so that it could be made explicit. No concept can be precisely known until a medium through which it can be discussed has been found. But the only possible terminology was one which sprang from the disciples' normal cast of mind, from their customary ways of thought and expression. Because they had been brought up on the Scriptures, they expressed this new and extraordinary fact, which was apparently so far removed from Jewish ideas, in expressions taken from the Scriptures. The Lord had already taught them to do this. The Law, the Prophets, and the Sapiential literature provided them with means of expression, which new content was to strain and crack.

There is thus a very long road from the call on the shore of Lake Genesareth to the gospel of John. There is an equally long road from the first preaching after Pentecost to the precise doctrine of Paul and John. The studies in this book are an attempt to retrace the steps by which the apostles became aware of their Master's divinity, to follow the hints, the proofs he himself gave them; to follow from book to book, from writer to writer, the evolution of the terms in which it came to be expressed. From the impression made on them by a distinguished Rabbi, from trust in the acknowledged Messiah, from the recognition of divine mystery living among them, they went on to accept the Lord as risen from the dead, as existing before all creation, as the Son of God, as God himself. That is God's amazing method of teaching, which led them from the hint of a mystery to the clear statement of belief in Jesus, Son of God.

The essays which follow need to be slowly and carefully read rather than hurriedly scanned. There is surely no better means of consolidating our faith than to come in contact with the experience of the apostles and through it with the work of the incarnate Lord.

The Expectation of God in the Old Testament

A. Gelin, P.S.S.

I

The Expectation of God in the Old Testament

A. Gelin, P.S.S.

THE MYSTERY OF Jesus Christ, God and man, is a part of the revelation of the New Testament. Messianic expectation —so various in its forms, so vigorous in growth, so transcendent in its history—was on this essential point far surpassed by a reality which was something entirely new. The prologue to Paul's Epistle to the Hebrews (1 : 1-3) attempts to express in solemn key and with restrained feeling mankind's astonishment before the unexpected wonder of the Son of God become man. It was as though the trail of faith which had wound its way through the Old Testament had suddenly emerged in a land till then unknown and undreamt of.

Messianic hope in the strict sense has as its object the coming of the Messiah as saviour. Israelite piety was irresistibly attracted by this Person, and represented him in various ways; but in none of them is he depicted as a divine being. The figure of the Messiah-King which was etched into the history of David's dynasty, and which in a later age was projected forward into the era of the Last Days, was not divine.[1] Nor was the Servant of Jahweh, the Prophet-Messiah of Deutero-Isaiah, who united in himself the characteristics of a new Moses and a new Jeremiah, and redeemed the world's sin by his martyrdom.[2] Nor was the

[1] The elements of a theory of the royal messianism with special reference to Psalm 2, will be found in E. Podechard, *Le Psautier, traduction littérale et explication historique*, (Lyon, 1948).

[2] This is the interpretation of A. Bentzen in *Messias, Moses redivivus*, (Zurich, 1948).

Son of Man seen in Daniel's vision, the loftiest symbol in biblical Judaism.[3]

This has not always been the attitude of exegetes. Indeed until relatively recently it was quite common to attempt to prove that the Old Testament did speak of the Messiah as God. The texts referred to have become well-known: Psalm 2:7; Psalm 45:8; Isaiah 9:6; Jeremiah 23:5; Micah 5:2; and the Jews were sometimes accused of obscuring or altering these clear statements. But reference to the important work of Ceuppens[4] will show how far we have come from that. There is in this work the punctiliously literal kind of interpretation advocated in *Divino Afflante Spiritu* (1943). Each text is set out without any special emphasis and, in Péguy's phrase, we can see 'the thin line of poplars' even though the 'castle with the four towers'—the gospels—is yet hidden.

The reason for such different interpretations of the same Old Testament texts is to be found in different notions of what prophecy is. Old Testament prophecies are sometimes regarded as a photograph of the future—'history in anticipation' according to Lesêtre; 'a clear preview of the Christ who was to come', says Bougaud; and de Broglie: 'a portrait which anticipates the future'. This attitude gives us a purely intellectual view of messianic hopes. It could lead us to set down two columns: on the left the texts of the Old Testament would be entered, usually without any immediate

[3]Cf. Lagrange, 'Les prophéties messianiques de Daniel', in *Revue Biblique* (1904), p. 494-520; G. Rinaldi, *Daniele,* (*Marietti,* Turin, 1947).

[4]Ceuppens, O. P., *De prophetiis messianicis in Antiquo Testamento* (Rome, 1935). See also a study which gives a rapid survey of the messianic hope, in H.P. de la Boullaye, S.J., *Jésus-Messie,* (Spes, Paris, 1930)—the fourth conference, p. 127-169, is called 'Le Témoinage des Prophètes'; and A. Gelin, *Key Concepts of the Old Testament,* (Eng. trans. Sheed & Ward).

reference to their historical context; and on the right, the corresponding texts of the New Testament. We could, however, forget that there will always be fewer entries in the left hand column, and that they will be less rich in content, although the expressions used may appear to be identical. We could also forget that what the Old Testament was striving to express was not simply a material fact; it was a religious dimension new to mankind, which had to be lived before it could adequately be proclaimed. Finally, we could forget that Messianic prophecy does not necessarily and formally imply prophecy of Christ.

Peter's second epistle compared the word of prophecy to those lamps of baked clay which provided light in dark places and were used by night watchmen until the break of dawn (1:20). He does not say that we must mistake the lamplight for day itself. The ancient messianic texts turn us in the direction of the Christ, they do not ever give us a description of him. To confuse our left hand column with the right by telescoping the two together, to confuse the time of God's patient waiting (Rom. 3:23) with the time of truth is to take no account of the ways of God. It is completely to misunderstand the slow progress and educative perspective of the old covenant.

A few examples will illustrate this. In Psalm 45:6 the Messiah is addressed thus: 'Your throne, O God, endures for ever and ever.' The use of the title *elohim* (i.e. God) would seem to demand the conclusion that 'the idea of a completely human Messiah gives way before the notion of a Messiah-God. Man was found to be too imperfect to bring the promised ideal to fruition. Therefore, Jahweh himself dons the mantle of the Messiah. The Messiah is still the king of Israel, still the descendant of David; but he is also the Lord, higher than the angels, the recipient of the adoration of the whole

universe.'⁵ This exaggerated opinion has been taken up from
another direction by a modern author, who considers that
'this title must be understood in its most literal sense'.⁶ But
this interpretation fails to take account of the *Sitz im Leben,*
the 'situation in life', whence the ancient royal poem, on
which the present text is based, derives; it refuses to admit
the technical use of the title *elohim* as a term of protocol—
the Bible applies it to any person whose position connoted
eminence : to leaders, for example, or judges, or Moses, or
the dynasty of David.⁷ We must agree with Ceuppens' conclusion that the title is applied to the king 'not because of his
divine dignity, but because of his dignity as king' and that it
would be better translated by a vaguer term like the Greek
theios or the Latin *divus,* i.e. 'your throne, man of God, is
for ever and ever'.⁸

A similar problem is to be found in Psalm 2 : 7 where the
Messiah-King recalls the day of his consecration and the
divine decree which defined his dignity. The decree envisaged is without question the ancient oracle preserved in 2
Samuel 7 where Jahweh binds himself to look upon every
king of David's house as his son and endows the dynasty with
an eternal character. The psalm was probably first intended
to be used at the enthronement of any member of the dynasty; but the significance of the word of Jahweh is not alt-
ered by the fact that it was then applied to the Messiah-
King alone :

I will tell of the decree of Jahweh :
He said to me, 'You are my son,
Today I have begotten you' (Psalm 2 : 7).

⁵Meignan, *David,* (Paris, 1899), p. 207.
⁶A. Feuillet, *Le Cantique des Cantiques,* (Paris, 1953), p. 219.
⁷R. Tournay, *Les Psaumes,* (Paris, 1950), p. 186, refers to Ex.
22:7; Ps. 82:6; Ex. 4:16 and 7:1; 1 Sam. 28:13; Zach. 12:8.
⁸Ceuppens, op. cit., p. 386.

The text is not concerned with the eternal generation of the Messiah, with his natural sonship, nor with his divinity, but with a begetting and a sonship in the metaphorical sense realized in adoption.[9]

Isaiah's messianism stems from the ancient kingly messianism; thus there is no reason to suppose that the oracle of Isaiah 9:1-6 affirms the 'divine nature' and 'divine attributes'[10] of the Messiah, who is referred to by the names

> Wonderful Counsellor, Mighty God,
> Everlasting Father, Prince of Peace.

The very length of this title is meant to indicate the standing of the one who bears it. The phrase 'Mighty God' could only have been understood in the sense of 'divine warrior'[11] in much the same sense as in Psalm 45.[12] Jeremiah also emphasizes the name of the Messiah. He calls him 'Jahweh-is-our-righteousness' in contrast to the reigning prince Zedikiah (cf. Jer. 23:6,; and this has led one scholar to conclude that 'the name of Jahweh thus given to the Messiah implies the divinity of this Messiah'.[13] If this argument were correct, what surprising conclusions could be drawn from other biblical names in which the name of Yahweh appears!

A new direction now appears in biblical tradition, which leads more closely to Christianity. When the messianic

[9]'Generatio nempe ad dignitatem regalem', Tournay, op. cit., p. 135-6. Cf. A. Robert, 'Considérations sur le messianisme du psaume 2', in *Recherches de science religieuse* (1951), p. 95.

[10]Lesêtre, article 'Jésus Christ', in *Dictionnaire de la Bible*, ed. Vigouroux, col. 1425, 1431; Ceuppens, op. cit., p. 237.

[11]J. Steinmann, *Le prophète Isaie*, (Cerf, Paris, 1950), p. 124.

[12]'The prophet's contemporaries... never considered attributing a divine nature strictly speaking to the Messiah'—Condamin, in *Le livre d'Isaïe*, (Paris, 1905), p. 58.

[13]Lesêtre, art. cit., col. 1425.

tradition and the sapiential current of thought met, they so
to speak fecundated each other, a process seen particularly in
the context of Proverbs 1-9, which we will not hesitate to call
the 'Protogospel of the Word'.[14] In these texts Wisdom is
described as having the characteristics of the Messiah, who
is a very real person. The proof of this will become apparent
from a comparison between Proverbs 8:14 and Isaiah
11:2, where the same attributes are used of both personal-
ities.[15] The endowment of Wisdom with the characteristics
of a real person greatly facilitated progress towards the idea
of a divine person, revealed to us precisely in his exercise of
the two authentically messianic activities, namely the judgement of the wicked and the inauguration of the reign of
moral perfection and happiness. Nonetheless, we cannot but
agree that the incarnation of the Wisdom of God is not yet
even suspected. And in spite of the deep learning and delicate
touch of the scholar who disagrees with this interpretation,
it is difficult to see how he can be right. The literary form of
'anthology'[16] could lead to Wisdom being presented as the
Spouse of Jahweh, as his Prophetess, as his Daughter even;
it could account for the fact that Messianic functions are
attributed to Wisdom; but it gives us no information about
the basic problem — whether Wisdom is to be considered a
real person, or whether it is merely a literary personification.

[14]A. Robert, 'Les attaches littéraires bibliques de Prov. 1-9', in
Revue Biblique, (1935), p. 525; cf. p. 523-524, 364; and, (1934), p.
187-188.
[15]Is. 11:2:
          'And the spirit of Jahweh shall rest upon him,
          The spirit of wisdom and *understanding*
          The spirit of *counsel* and *might,*
          The spirit of knowledge and fear of Jahweh.'
Prov. 8:14: 'I (Wisdom) have *counsel* and sound wisdom, *understanding and might.'*
[16]With regard to this procedure, see A. Gelin, *Problèmes de
l'Ancien Testament,* (Lyon, 1952), p. 105.

The first alternative would be selected only by a Christian interpreter.

There is a magnificently poetic passage in the book of Baruch (3:38) where Wisdom is pictured coming down from heaven to live among men, bearing all the character-istics of the Jewish Law :

Now it has appeared on earth
And mixed freely among men.

Some of the Fathers saw in this verse a hint of the incarna-tion. But this is to endow the text with overtones it does not possess; because the context is so clear, there is general agree-ment on this point. Yet those somewhat overdrawn inter-pretations bear witness not only to the Christian amazement at the event, which is the basis of our faith; they were drawn only because of the rich possibilities of the ancient texts, in which we can detect what seem to be mysterious embryonic movements of future revelations.[17]

This is particularly true of the title Son of Man, which can be seen emerging with the apocalyptic book of Daniel in the second half of the second century B.C. Daniel was given an extraordinary vision in which a being 'like a son of man' appeared moving on the clouds of heaven. The apparition

[17]This is the meaning of Fr. D. Condamin's observation already quoted in note 12. With reference to Isaiah 9:6, he says: 'this mes-sianic title (Mighty God) like all other prophecies, when fulfilled was realized in a more perfect sense than was understood by the prophet's contemporaries. They knew nothing of the mystery of the Trinity, and so when they distinguished between Jahweh and the Messiah to come, they had no intention of giving him a divine nature.' Recent discussions on the spiritual sense have led critics (e.g. J. Coppens) to ask whether the prophet himself might not have had a charismatic revelation which would have put him in advance of his hearers. This would have the merit of preserving the the 'literal' sense of Is. 9:6 advocated by Ceuppens, Robert (*Revue Biblique,* 1934, p. 188), Condamin, and Fischer.

moved towards God and received a commission to judge all
things and to have dominion eternally (7 : 13). The symbolism of the vision is then explained by the interpreting
angel as a reference to the eschatological Israel, 'the people
of the saints', who will be suffused with power from on high
to continue the struggle against the four Monsters, symbolic
of the pagan empires (18 : 27). But just as these empires are
represented by the kings who rule over them, so also perhaps,
in Daniel's mind, the kingdom of the saints is represented by
its king, the Messiah. Recent studies on corporate personality will possibly lead to a better appreciation of the ambiv-
alence of the title Son of Man.[18] Jewish tradition, however,
became firmly attached to the former aspect, namely the
Son of Man as a person, and we have some indications from
the recent discoveries at Qumrân that the idea was preva-
lent during the first century before Christ. The parables
of Henoch, usually dated at about this time, describe a
'supernatural being unlike anyone in the world'. Like Wisdom, this being pre-exists close to God from whom he has
received all gifts, and the special commission to save all men
and to judge the nations before reigning for ever with the
just. His names are Messiah, the Supreme Just One, the
Chosen, and above all, the Son of Man.[19]

It would be impossible to maintain that a relationship of
fatherhood or nature existed between God and this unknown
but sublime being, yet we are forced to agree that there is no
person more perfect in all pre-Christian Jewish messianism.

[18]A single person can represent the unity of a given group,
so that there exists between individual and group a fluid relationship. This idea has been explained by Wheeler Robinson, A.
Stanley Cook, O. Eissfeldt and J. Pederson. See *Biblica*, (1952),
p. 460-463.

[19]*Book of Henoch*, (Eng. trans. and ed. R. H. Charles, in *Epigrapha and Pseudo-epigrapha of the Old Testament*, [Oxford,
1913]). The most relevant passages on the Son of Man are quoted
later, in P. Benoit's essay, p. 85-6.

This figure, we may note, takes on the characteristics of all the types we have been examining. He has the characteristics of the Servant of Jahweh,[20] as well as those of the Messiah-King. In this connexion, the interpretation of Psalm 110 by the Jewish community of Alexandria is very significant. This ancient poem was probably first recited in David's honour[21]; after the downfall of the dynasty it was transposed to an eschatological setting, and celebrated the enthronement of the Messiah-King in Zion : but the Septuagint transfers the scene to heaven, in the midst of angels, where the Messiah-King has always existed, as the adopted and especially loved son of God—

> Jahweh said to my lord :
> 'Sit at my right hand. . . .
> The might in the day of your power is yours
> In the splendour of the saints,
> Before the day star, from the womb I begot you.'

This 'revised' reading seems to belong to the same climate of ideas as the book of Daniel :[22] not all the details are clear, but at least it is quite clear that contemporary Judaism was attuned to expect a heavenly and transcendent being; and this gives an added significance to Christ's reply to the court of the Sanhedrin when he referred both to Psalm 110 and Daniel 7 in the same breath.

But there is still no suggestion that the Messiah is divine. The scholar striving to trace the course of the messianic hope gathers the impression that he is simply given no clue of the

[20]Hen. 48:4—'he will be the light of the nations'—compare Isaiah 42:6 and 49:6.

[21]E. Podechard, 'Psaume 110', in *Etudes de critique et d'histoire religieuses*, (Lyon, 1948), p. 7-24.

[22]Lagrange refers to this climate of ideas in *Revue Biblique*, (1905), p. 48-50.

wonder towards which it leads. He might well ask, was there any less difficulty in grasping it in Jesus' time?

Israel clearly did not expect a Messiah-God. What they did expect was something broader. The whole Old Testament faith is directed to this wider theme, which is what gives unity to all its various strands. This theme is the coming of God.[23]

The constant attitude of the people of God was one of prayer and hope; their gaze was for ever fixed on the future; that is to say, they were constantly calling for the coming of God, constantly ready to welcome it : and this was because God himself had revealed to them the secret of this expectation. The name Jahweh held no metaphysical secret, but something far more precious for the life of the chosen People; it enshrined a sort of divine dynamic. Jahweh means 'He is', a name understood in three ways, none of them mutually exclusive (Exodus 3 : 13-15). 'He is' the only God who matters compared with other gods—they are seen to be non-beings. 'He is' with his people, a statement which finds its truest significance in the narrative of Exodus, and then impregnates the atmosphere of the whole Bible.[24] Finally 'He is' always 'on the ball'. We claim indulgence for this colloquial expression, which is adapted from Eichrodt's phrase,[25] and admirably expresses the character of the God of the Old Testament : the God of battles, of righteousness i.e. of powerful interventions—of punishment. This God leads history to its conclusion by involving himself in it, and inserting into it those 'days of Jahweh'—the manifestations of his pleasure or his anger—which are key points in a history

[23]G. Pidoux, 'Le Dieu qui vient', in *Cahiers théologiques de l'actualité protestante,* no. 17 (Delachaux and Niestlé, 1947).

[24]Exod. 3:12; see Judges 6:12 which takes up this phraseology.

[25]'Er ist wirklich und wahrhaftig da', in *Theologie des Alten Testaments,* (Berlin, 1950), vol. 1, p. 88.

moving towards its Last Day. Three phrases culled from contemporary scholars pin-point this motivating force in the spiritual life of Israel. L. H. Bleeker writes : 'the name Jahweh has a powerful eschatological significance'; 'when you know God' says Eichrodt, 'you also know the coming of God'; and according to Pidoux, 'his final triumph is an eschatological necessity'.

Certain 'days of Jahweh' were preserved in Israel's memory; and each of them was a coming of God, a theophany, which moulded the course of history. Here or there, unexpectedly, in different places (like the ark of the Covenant, always on the move), Jahweh showed himself : he showed himself in certain phenomena—storm, cloud, fire, thunder and trumpet-blast—which expressed the sudden, gratuitous, mysterious, transcendent nature of his coming. The first of these, and model of all the rest, was the primordial theophany of Sinai. So he comes for the conquest of Canaan :

Lord, when you went forth from Seir,
when you marched from the region of Edom,
the earth trembled,
and the heavens deluged rain (Judges 5 : 4).

Again he comes from the south against the Chaldeans in the sixth century :

God came from Teman,
and the Holy One from Mount Paran.
His glory was like a great light,
And from his hand the lightning flashed (Habakkuk 3 : 3).

Later he appeared to decimate the pagan nations :

> Behold the name of Jahweh comes from afar
> burning with anger (Isaiah 30 : 27).

and to correct his own people :

> Behold, Jahweh is leaving his house
> He comes down and overwhelms
> the proud men of earth (Michaeas 1 : 3).

The promise of relief from the extreme hardships of Exile came to a fallen Israel in these words :

> Say to those who are of a fearful heart,
> 'Be strong, fear not !
> Behold your God
> will come with vengeance;
> he will come in person and save you' (Isaiah 35 : 4).

The final 'coming' of Jahweh is proclaimed in the psalms of the Kingdom which were sung in the temple liturgy after the return from Babylon.[26] The overture to the founding of the Kingdom of Jahweh, a kingdom of peace, justice and intimate knowledge of God, is in the form of an apocalypse, a colossal fanfare of strange instruments. The forces of the universe are alerted to welcome the King now at hand, like Sinai on a cosmic scale :

> With trumpets and the sound of the horn
> Make a joyful noise before Jahweh, come only our King!
> Let the sea roar and all that fills it;
> the world and those who dwell in it.

[26]Psalms 93, 96, 99. These psalms depend largely on the Deutero-Isaiah and speak of the definitive rule of Jahweh which will come about in the Last Days. They speak as though the Last Days were actually present.

Let the floods clap their hands,
Let the hills sing for joy together
Before Jahweh, for he comes
to rule the earth.
He will judge the world with justice
And the peoples with equity (Psalm 98:6-9).

This passage is worth comment for the care with which an attempt has been made to express a deep truth. The universal invitation and the magnificent appearance of God both leave the underlying mystery untouched. It is in the nature of theophanies to be incomprehensible, indescribable. How will the final, conclusive and altogether exceptional appearance come about? Jahweh had once said to Moses (Exodus 33:20): 'You can never see my face, because no man can see me and live', and the last coming of God is similarly described by Malachi 3:2: 'But who can endure the day of his coming, and who can stand when he appears?'[27] That atmosphere of holy dread is felt always when God summoned the ancient writers and allowed them to approach very close to the mystery of the Last Days. Never giving his name, never even giving an exact picture, they nevertheless in the darkness of faith testified to the One who would come into the world, Jesus Christ.

Catholic liturgy delights in contrast. On the feast of the Presentation in the Temple, the lesson from Malachi describes the entry of Jahweh into his Temple. The dominant mood is triumph, the imagery is magnificent in this, the last page of the Old Testament. But then the gospel is heard, of two Galileans carrying their child to the Temple in obedience

[27]Exod. 33:20; Mal. 3:2.

to the Law. They are very ordinary, little people. They
choose the humblest kind of ceremonial. The officiating
priest carries out his duty without realizing that Jahweh had
at last really entered his Temple. There lies the mood of the
New Testament, a feeling of 'the humility of God' when he
said: 'Behold I am come' (Hebrews 10:9). The feeling is
caught very aptly in this short verse :

Trumpets, lightning; earth shudders.
But when you came down to the Virgin's womb
Not a sound was heard.[28]

And so in Jesus Christ, God one day became man. He was
a man who really felt thirsty on the roads of Samaria, who
really wept at Lazarus' tombside, who felt himself crushed in
the garden of agony, and who suffered on the cross. We
mentioned at the beginning that the incarnation had not
been expected by the Old Testament, and so the Jews set
themselves against it, because such a fact seemed so impos-
sibly hard to credit. But now God had displayed his plan.
The appearance of the Word made flesh cast a light into the
alleyways where hope had been groping its slow way along.[29]
It drew the theme of the coming of God to a miraculous
conclusion. It gave the theophanies of old[30] the value of
'figures', pointers; it gave meaning to all those incidents in
which Jahweh had appeared in human guise. These

[28]Budé (editor), *Anthologie Palatine,* vol. 1, no. 37.
[29]'When the Saviour had come to us and had given a body to
the Gospel, then he brought it about that everything should become like his Gospel.' Origen, *In Joannem,* vol. 1, no. 8.
[30]'Omnes apparitiones Veteris Testamenti ad illam appari-
tionem ordinatæ fuerunt, qua Filius Dei apparuit in carne.' *Summa
Theologiae,* ad 1, qu. 51, art. 2. This text speaks of angelic apparitions; we may include among these the appearances of the 'angel
of Jahweh', a substitute for Jahweh himself.

'anthropomorphisms' and 'anthropopathisms' have only recently been studied in detail.[31] The Bible speaks of the mouth, eyes, ears, nose, and the feet of God, of his intercourse with men, his anger, his pity, his repentance and his laughter. This method of expression was adopted to press home the fact that Jahweh is a living God. 'God himself', says W. Vischer, 'smashes the abstract images and concepts which men use to describe him, and brings them face to face with himself as a living person. He does not appear as a thought or a lofty idea in the minds of those to whom he reveals himself, but rather as a friend or enemy of the most intimate and the most personal kind.' This anthropomorphism runs right through the Bible, and is never an indication of a less spiritual view of God. And today we can see that there was something providential in this—a figurative anticipation of what was to come, a silent prophecy, as if God's design had been 'to give man a hidden foretaste of his incarnation'.[32]

[31]Anthropopathism is the literary device which predicates human feelings of God; cf. F. Michaeli, *Dieu à l'image de l'homme, étude de la notion anthropomorphique de Dieu dans l'ancien Testament,* (Paris, 1950).

[32]A. Chollet, summarizing Thomassin, in 'Anthropomorphisme' *Dict. de Théologie Catholique,* col. 1368.

Christ Jesus in the Apostolic Church

J. Schmitt

II

Christ Jesus in the Apostolic Church

J. Schmitt

THE APOSTOLIC CHURCH first expressed its faith in Jesus, the divine Messiah, through preaching and worship. In its preaching the church brings to light the numerous evangelical and scriptural sources of its faith; it expresses its rich potentialities, its varied themes and aspects, the multiplicity of formulae through which it was transmitted : it communicates something of the religious and moral tone of that faith, its liturgical and in some respects ritualistic flavour; and finally, it shows us clearly how this faith, the faith in the divinity of Jesus, gradually came to dominate the whole thought of the growing church. But the first question to answer is, how do we know what this primitive faith was? what traces of it can still be found?

A.   THE SOURCES

We could, to begin with, call upon the most primitive strata of the gospel tradition; but they would be of little help here, primarily because their subject—the theme of salvation—is not our concern, and also because of the way in which they were re-written by the first and second generations of Christians. Two categories of texts now remain to us, both different in character, both of apostolic origin, and both of the highest importance for our study. They are firstly the catechetical discourses recorded in the first part of Acts[1]

[1]Cf. Acts 2:14-40; 3:12-26; 4:8-12; 5:29-32; 7:2-53; 10:34-43; 13:15-41. (These are the main discourses of Acts referred to.) Compare with 8:26-40.

and secondly the formulas of belief and prayer preserved in the epistles, notably those of Paul.[2]

These various fragments stand out from their context as being more or less archaic both in content and in form; unlike the rest of the New Testament they belong to the earliest strata of the apostolic writings, and thus tell us something about the faith in Christ, if not at the very beginning, at least long before the composition of, for example, the synoptic gospels.

The Historicity of the Discourses

The value of these documents taken as a whole is a matter of some discussion. Indeed, the historical character of the discourses in Acts continues to provide a battlefield for violently conflicting opinions. Are they, on the one hand, brief summaries of the 'witness' Peter and the apostles, Stephen and the seven deacons bore to Christ in the circumstances pictured by Luke? Do they truly reproduce specific examples of the earliest preaching in Jerusalem and Palestine? Or are they, on the other hand, to a greater or less degree, free adaptations made by the author of Acts in his desire to embellish the narrative with speeches put into the mouths of his leading characters in the style of classical Greek and Roman historians? The conflicting points of view revealed in these two questions are as old as the critical study of Acts itself, and embody two equally outlandish notions of the sources used by Luke; yet they continue to dominate the discussion and research of many scholars even today. These ideas owe their comparative strength at present largely to a slavish conservatism which is the main reason why the over

[2]Cf. 1 Cor. 15:3-5; 12:3; 16:22; Rom. 10:9; 1:3-4; Phil. 2:6-11; Eph. 5:14; 1 Tim. 3:16. Compare with 1 Pet. 2:1-10; 2:21-25; Apoc. 22:20.

hasty conclusions of the older school of literary criticism persist in contemporary exegesis.

But a clearer understanding of the structure and pre-history of Luke's text has given a new direction to studies of Acts and a more valid and objective view of the origin and the meaning of our documents has begun to emerge, an approach which is more balanced and more accurate. This approach, differing from both those which had become almost traditional, stresses the fact that in spite of Luke's editorial activity, the discourses of Peter and other disciples, especially those in Chapters two to ten, are based on various apostolic sources, of various dates, but all of them early. This means that their contents and even, on the whole, their form have a real historical value. Thus, they not only reproduce the main themes of the oral gospel: scriptural, doctrinal, moral and religious; but they also show how the same message of salvation was adapted to different audiences by different preachers in various forms.[3] These fragments therefore are of major importance from several points of view. Brief and summary though they are, they enable us to see the essential elements of the primitive Christian creed, and how these were expressed in certain apostolic circles.

But there is yet more. These documents are obviously early, but it does not seem possible to fix their precise date; nevertheless, one can see in them a definite development—a development which is all the more striking in that it does not compromise the continuity of the faith, but protects and strengthens it. Two texts of Petrine origin are particularly

[3]An example of the sort of preaching given to the Jews in Jerusalem can be seen in the catechetical fragments in Chapters three to five; for the preaching to the Palestinian proselytes, see Chapter 10; Stephen's speech in Chapter 7 gives us the style of hellenist preachers of the Alexandrian diaspora; and for that of the Asian diaspora, see Philip's instruction to the Ethiopian in 8:30-38.

informative on this point. There is firstly Peter's address in
the Temple—one of the most primitive fragments of the
New Testament—which records the preaching of the
apostles in its earliest known form (3 : 12-26); secondly there
is Peter's instruction to Cornelius which gives evidence of a
far more highly developed thought (10 : 34-43). The latter
actually introduces, for the first time, themes which were
later given a key place in Mark, the oldest of the gospels as
we have them now. Yet, when all allowances have been
made for the very real differences in approach, form and
subject-matter, there is no doubt that both these texts do
transmit a belief in salvation achieved by Jesus, the divine
Messiah.

The Historicity of the Formulas of Faith

The formulas or brief summaries of faith of a liturgical
and didactic character found in the epistles give rise to the
kind of questions we discussed in the last section. They are
hieratic in tone, even composed according to the rules of
early Christian prosody;[4] their vocabulary is quite peculiar,
and their content too is characteristic—a rather recapitula-
tive treatment of the theme of salvation. All these characteristics clearly indicate a literary form easily recognized as
completely original. But we may well ask how this unique
literary form came into being. Are the formulas earlier than
the different texts in which we find them embodied? Do
they go back to the first communities in Palestine and the
earliest pagan-Christian communities? Or alternatively, by
analogy with other New Testament writings, are they the
work of the authors in whose name they stand, whose writings show with what mastery they could use the hieratic style

[4]Particularly the rhythmic structure achieved by parallelism,
antithesis, and climax, and the use of relative clauses and parti-
ciples.

to emphasize the vital points in their message and the climaxes of their thought?[5] In other words they may be either relics of the many catechetical and prayer formulas through which the apostles first communicated their beliefs; or they may actually only be evidence of the creative brilliance of a few preachers of a later generation.

The only means we have of choosing with any degree of certainty the more correct alternative is by comparing the literary and doctrinal keynotes of the formulas, first of all with their immediate context, and then with the parallel fragments of Acts. However, the results of such a comparison are not always conclusive. For instance, is the hymn to Jesus, the Lord, in the Epistle to the Philippians (2:5b-11) of Palestinian origin, or is it a highly original poem of Paul's composition? Scholars remain sharply divided over this point. I opt for the Palestinian origin of the hymn because its contents and style seem to me more akin to Palestinian formulas of faith and prayer than to the set pieces of hieratic writing stamped with the hallmark of Paul.

B. The Characteristics of the Faith of the Apostolic Church

The first basic conclusion we arrive at through a study of the sources we have mentioned is this, that even in the earliest texts the most important single element in the life of the new-born church was faith in Jesus, Messiah and divine Saviour. It would not be too much to say that this was its inheritance from the Master, and the principle of its life. In the earliest records of the apostolic faith—Peter's address in the Temple (Acts 3:12-26) or the prayer of the community in Jerusalem (4:24-30)—there is no indication that this

[5]Examples of this unusual style can be found in passages such as these: 1 Cor. 13:1-13; Eph. 1:3ff; 1:15ff; 1 Pet. 1:13-22, 25.

faith was just then being invented or that it was being elaborated. Contrary to the view still favoured by certain critics, the Christians of the first generation did not 'create' faith in Jesus to provide some kind of cult worship of their own, and in this way to hasten the separation of Christians from Judaism. Faith in Christ stood at the very source of the first apostolic community.

Two questions immediately arise from this. The first, what is the source of this faith in Christ? the second, what are its overriding characteristics? Without pausing to go into the interpretation of the actual texts, we may briefly sum up the information they give on these two points.

Its origins

The Jerusalem Church's faith in Christ sprang from a threefold source: the paschal event, the gospel facts, and Old Testament texts.

Risen from the dead, that is to say 'raised to the right hand of God', Jesus was seen to possess 'glory' and 'power', 'might', 'dominion', 'sovereignty'. In other words, he shares with his Father attributes which are strictly divine. This might not have denoted any more than a unity of function between God and Christ; but, as the apostolic writings indicate, these qualities had come to have a spiritual significance in certain Jewish circles; and therefore this unique prerogative of Christ implied for the first generation of Christians not only unity of function but, so to speak, community of condition.

But the faith of the apostles and their disciples was not confined to that fact alone. They began a re-appraisal of the gospel history in the light of the resurrection, and with sudden insight they saw Jesus' humble life and his suffering as no more than an initial, incomplete, and mysteriously veiled hint at his true status as Son of God. They saw them as an overture to the grand paschal revelation. The Master's life on earth points unmistakably to the resurrection as his destiny from the moment he assumed the mantle of Messiah in the Jordan. Without the exaltation of Jesus, his taking flesh would have been an event without meaning. There is no clash between the revelation of himself in Galilee and his exaltation in glory. The Lord who 'sits at the right hand' of the Father continually bears witness to the Christ of gospel history—bears witness that the two are one.

In order to justify this kind of re-appraisal of the gospel ministry, the apostles and the other bearers of the good news were not content merely with adducing the Master's miraculous deeds. True, they presented the latter usually as 'wonders', 'signs', 'acts of supreme power'[6] and also considered that their own miracles, currently being worked 'in the Lord Jesus' name', were of equal value.[7] Nevertheless, as the many apostolic writings testify, the apostles also appealed to the teaching of Christ (for which they show a marked predilection), in particular to the 'scriptures' through which the Master had pointed out what he was and whence he had come. If we postpone until the next contribution to this book consideration of Daniel 7 : 13-14, on the Messiah as Son of Man, which is seen at its clearest in the mouth of the martyred Stephen (Acts 7 : 56), we are left with four texts of scripture whose penetrating influence is felt not only in all the discourses in Acts but also in the formulas found in the epistles, and these texts go a long way to account for the latter's characteristics and form. The four texts are, firstly, the poems on the suffering and glorified Servant of Jahweh in Isaiah, particularly the poem in 52 : 13—53 : 12;[8] secondly there is the fragment in Deuteronomy (18 : 15-19)

[6]Cf. Acts 2:22; 10:38.
[7]Cf. Acts 3:6; 3:12-13; 3:16; 4:29-30; 5:12; 5:15-16.
[8]Cf. Acts 3:12-16; 4:27-28; 8:30-38; Phil. 2:6-11; 1 Cor. 15:3.

describing the 'prophet' like Moses whom Jahweh promises
to send to his people;[9] thirdly verse 1 of Psalm 110, which
speaks of the Messiah as 'the Lord who sits at the right hand
of Jahweh';[10] and finally Psalm 118:22 concerning 'the
stone rejected by the builders' which has become 'the chief
cornerstone'.[11]

The synoptics put all this scriptural evidence in Jesus'
mouth, as his way of drawing attention to the fact that he
was the Messiah. Psalm 110:1 provided the theme for discussion with the scribes about the Messiah as 'Son of
David',[12] and the same text lay behind the great declaration he made to the High Priest[13] during his trial before the
Sanhedrin. Similarly, the Master quoted the text of Psalm
118 as a final barbed, anti-Jewish thrust by way of conclusion to the story of the unfaithful vine-dressers.[14] The
Servant of Jahweh poems are the sources on which he drew
for his prophecies of his passion and glorification.[15] The
Deuteronomic fragment can be identified as the source
underlying the different lessons by which he strove to pin-
point the nature of his work, as he in turn compared and
contrasted it with that of Moses.[16] In each case, Christ's
use of the scriptures prepared the way, point for point, for
the scriptural arguments used by the apostles and their disciples. There is a view, less common now than formerly,
which regards all these texts as fraudulently put into the

[9]Cf. Acts 3:22-23; 7:37.
[10]Cf. Acts 2:33-36; 5:31; Phil. 2:9-11; 1 Cor. 12:3; 16:22; Rom.
10:9.
[11]Cf. Acts 4:11-12.
[12]Cf. Mk. 12:35-37; Matt. 22:41-46; Lk. 20:41-44.
[13]Cf. Mk. 14:62; Matt. 26:64; Lk. 22:69.
[14]Cf. Mk. 12:10-11; Matt. 21:42; Lk. 20:17.
[15]Cf. Mk. 8:31 and parallels; 9:31 and parallels; 10:33-34 and
parallels; and Lk. 22:37 compared with Mk. 15:34 and parallels.
[16]Cf. Mk. 7:10 and parallels; 10:1-12 and parallels. Cf. Matt.
5:1 ff.

mouth of Christ in a desperate attempt to reconcile his teaching with what the apostles were preaching. But these texts belong to the earliest stratum of synoptic tradition, and by their richness and rightness they convey the whole tone of the gospel teaching in general; so that there can be no doubt that they do represent the most fundamental elements of the teaching which the first Christians received from Christ himself. They truly highlight the continuity between the gospel teaching and the emergent faith in Jesus, Messiah, Saviour and God.

Its development

What we have said must not be taken to mean that the faith of the apostles was from the very beginning fully aware of all the implications of the gospel revelation. That was certainly not the case. The differences of thought and language in the various texts of Acts and Paul show that although faith in Christ was present from the very beginning, nevertheless it was marked—especially among the first generation Christians— by a growing awareness of the mystery of Jesus, the mystery of his perfect condition, the mystery of his real Sonship of God. There are three distinguishing features in this deepening insight.

First, although belief in Christ already occupied first place in the thought and devotion of the faithful, it only gradually became the central point in the expression of primitive faith. The most ancient texts actually leave us with the very clear impression that what struck the disciples most of all in the glorification of their Master and in their own spiritual experience was the revelation that salvation was achieved. They realized that the kingdom of God was now established in all its fullness; in particular, they realized that Israel had now been restored to its condition of God-governed Assembly or

Church, purified and sanctified by the Spirit. These were the ideas which first occupied the minds of the Jewish Christians.

Hence, we are not surprised to discover that in the discourses of Peter in the Temple and before the Sanhedrin (Acts 3 : 12-26 and 4 : 8-12; cf. 5 : 29-32), the preaching of Christ Jesus is completely dominated by the theme of redemption regained. This is clear from the tone of the passages and from the context in which they occur, both of which are distinctly messianic; and it emerges even more clearly from the fact that Christ is presented as the unique, heavenly Saviour. This is significant from two points of view. It indicates on the one hand that in the primitive faith, belief in the divine status of Jesus was in a sense secondary to the theme of the inauguration of the 'last days' of Jahweh. From another aspect, it suggests unmistakably that the chief object of doctrinal reflection at that time was not Jesus in himself, but the salvation which he brought.

But the disciples soon became aware of the divine prerogatives of their glorified Master and of his role as saviour; they began to see more clearly the difference between the Christian salvation and the Jewish order of things. And when this happened their faith in Christ Jesus became so central that it overshadowed even the belief in the 'last days'. This precision is, as we have said, not so much a theological development as a growing awareness of the implications of the gospel message and the paschal event. On the one hand, emphasis was laid on the identity between the Christ of history and the Saviour exalted in glory; and on the other hand his relationship with God was more clearly expressed. The principal result of this theological reflection is summed up in the theme of the Lord, the Son pre-existing with the Father.

Our sources, fragments of prayer and preaching, do not give the full picture of this theological development. The

first generation of Christians was really more concerned with
living the faith than with worrying about how to translate
it into neat themes written in faultless theological language.
Furthermore, even though the formulas that we have are
rich in implications, they communicate only an imperfect
impression of the ideas current in the communities which
composed and recited them. These formulas were composed
primarily for liturgical purposes, and there is always a slight
gap between liturgical prayer and theological thought.
Moreover, they were composed for the most part in Jewish
Christian circles, and this accounts for their tendency to
proclaim the faith in the divinity of Jesus only indirectly,
rather than in explicit terms.

Its richness

In spite of the sporadic and unpolished way in which the
new born faith in the divinity of Christ was expressed, it was
nevertheless distinguished by a rich variety of points of view;
a variety it owed to the fact that it had so many different
sources, all of equal importance, to draw on. This was never
true to the same extent in any later age. The faith gained in
depth, its varied points of view were moulded into a single
synthesis; but in the process individual aspects which had
previously been important in their own right now lost their
individuality and, above all, lost their biblical savour. If we
grasp the characteristic features of the faith of this age, we
will appreciate its freshness and originality, and see how
deeply rooted it was in the Old Testament and the gospel
message.

C. The Main Themes

The best way for us to define what the original belief in
Christ meant is by dwelling on the different titles given to

the risen Master by his apostles and their disciples. Prompted by the teaching of the Master himself who, in turn, drew them from the Scriptures, these titles, because of their scriptural basis, with the new shades of meaning that attached to it, are in a certain sense a summary of the primitive Christian faith.

'The Prophet' (Deut. 18 : 15-19)

The title of Prophet, one of the most archaic and probably one of the earliest of the names given Christ by the different groups in the Jerusalem community, was lifted immediately from the passage in Deuteronomy which speaks of 'the Prophet', a second Moses, whom God would raise up to save Israel :

> Jahweh, your God, will raise up for you
> a prophet like me (Moses) from among you
>   my brethren,
> to him you must listen. . . .
> And Jahweh said to me
> 'All they have said, has been said rightly.
> I will raise up for them a prophet like you from among
> their number; my words will be put on his lips;
> what he speaks to them shall only be
> what I command him to say' (Deut. 18 : 15, 18).

Note the place of supreme importance given to this text in the earliest preaching. Stephen's speech—which typifies the hellenist preaching to the Jews of Jerusalem and Palestine —uses it in a messianic sense (Acts 7 : 37); and it seems to have been used as an introduction to the series of scripture texts marshalled by Peter in his sermon in the Temple :

> For heaven must detain him (the risen Jesus) until the time of universal renewal of which God spoke in ancient

times through his holy prophets. For Moses said : 'Jahweh will raise up for you from among your brethren a prophet like me. . . . And whoever does not listen to that prophet shall be destroyed from the people' (Acts 3 : 21-23; cf. v. 25).

Thus, of all the scriptural testimonies used by the early church, this is the most basic. Many different forms of apostolic preaching use it as their common source.

In Peter's discourse as well as in Stephen's, it is adduced in support of the closely related themes of 'the last days' and the Church. (In this connexion a comparison between Acts 3 : 19-26 and 7 : 35 ff. is instructive.) The ancient faithless Israel is now thrown into opposition with the new 'People of God', faithful and pure; more particularly, Moses the founder and lawgiver of the first God-governed community has a new counterpart in Christ, the architect of the messianic Assembly. There was an idea dear to the first church in Jerusalem that the final salvation properly speaking would consist of a restoration of that first theocracy of Moses' time, and this notion became quite naturally the context of the title 'Prophet' as applied to Jesus. It suggested in one bold stroke the significance of the title, for Christ had been acclaimed restorer of the completed and perfected Kingdom of God in virtue of the saving work he accomplished through his Cross and his Gospel Message.

'Servant and Son' (Isaiah 52 : 13—53 : 12)

The poems in Isaiah on the theme of the suffering and glorified 'Servant of Jahweh' quite clearly provided the inspiration for Jesus' predictions of his own passion and resurrection. They also dominated, almost to the exclusion of all other ideas, the disciples' doctrinal and religious thought. There are five or more passages among the very few traces of the prayer and preaching of the apostles, which, while by no means identical, are nevertheless closely related in thought and style, and these passages reproduce the texts of Isaiah more or less word for word.

Peter's address in the Temple begins and ends on the theme of 'Jesus the Servant', 'raised' (in other words 'glorified') by God, and thus made 'the Christ', the saviour of Israel, the architect and initiator of 'the renewal of all things' : [17]

> Men of Israel, said Peter, why do you wonder at this (the healing of the lame man)?. . . . The God of Abraham, and of Isaac, and of Jacob, the God of our father, glorified his servant Jesus, whom you delivered up and denied in the presence of Pilate. . . . God raised up his servant and sent him to you first of all, to bless you and turn every one of you from your evil ways (Acts 3 : 12-26).

Paul has the same teaching. In his first epistle to the Corinthians he quotes the 'tradition' he had received—probably shortly after his conversion; and according to this: 'Christ died for our sins, *according to the Scriptures*' (1 Cor. 15 : 36). In spite of its summary nature, this text clearly alludes to the passage in Isaiah (52 : 13—53 : 12) on the passion of the 'Servant' regarded as a source of 'reconciliation' for sinners. The narrative which describes Philip's instruction to the Ethiopian similarly underlines the fact that in this particular case the Gospel took the form of a commentary on chapter 53, v. 7-8 of Isaiah which speaks of the obedience of the 'Servant' in undergoing his suffering. [18]

There are finally two passages even more suggestive than

[17] Acts 3. Verse 13a explains verse 26; the resurrection of Jesus was the entry into glory given him by God.
[18] Acts 8:26-40, especially 30-35.

these. The prayer of the Community at Jerusalem repro-
duced in Acts 4 : 24-30 has a deeply religious and, in a sense,
liturgical atmosphere. In its leading ideas, it was evidently
inspired by the same Book of the Servant in Isaiah :

.... for truly in this city there were gathered together
against your anointed servant Jesus, both Herod and
Pontius Pilate, with the Gentiles and the peoples of Israel,
to do whatever your power and your wisdom had pre-
destined to take place.[19]

Another, even more completely scriptural in tone, is found
in the hymn to the 'humiliated' and 'exalted' Christ, preserved in the letter to Philippi, chapter 2 : 6-11. We have
already mentioned the likely origin of this text in Palestine,
and it seems to be, both in form and content, a remarkably
close reproduction of the text of Isaiah on the humiliated and
glorified Servant. Seldom do we find a biblical text so lumin-
ously and so accurately interpreted for us by the apostolic
Church.

However, although the earliest communities of Christians
found in Isaiah the aptest formulas expressive of their faith
in Christ, they did not fail to point out that Jesus, because
of his true status in heaven, and even on earth, fulfils the
ancient ideal of the 'Servant' in an unexpected way, and even
surpassed it. In their minds, the passage of Isaiah 52 : 13—
53 : 12 taken together with the other fragments more or less
parallel to it, had a basic religious importance, because it
bore witness to the value of the cross as expiation for sin. But
more than that, these texts were taken as a proof that the
Just One becomes, through his redeeming passion, the
author and the ideal of a new, sanctified, human race; and
this finally supplied a connexion with the title 'Leader' (Acts

[19]Note also the parallels with Is. 61:1 and Ps. 2:2.

4

3 : 15; 5 : 31) (*Archégos*) which was given to Christ by some of the early communities.

But the real interest of these texts lies in their doctrinal value. The disciples used these titles to clarify their idea of what their Master really was. Jesus, like the Just One envisaged by the Prophet (Is. 53 : 11), was the innocent, sinless victim, laden with the infidelities of Israel; he could, therefore, be called the Just One (*o Dikaios*) in the fullest sense of the word.[20] Moreover, because he was, like the Servant,[21] anointed with the Spirit, that is with God's own creative, saving power,[22] therefore he could be called thereafter the Holy One (*o Agios*)[23] and above all, the Christ (*o Christos*).[24]

These titles are primarily messianic; and now, summing them all up, specifying their precise meaning and adding further depth to that meaning, there is the more basic title, 'Servant of God' (*Pais Theou*).[25] The disciples pondered on this title in the light of the gospel revelation, and in applying it to Jesus they gave it a new meaning. They began by developing two minor themes of Isaiah's, the 'delight of Jahweh' in his Servant,[26] and the willing obedience of the Servant of Jahweh.[27] They then insisted that the relationship between Christ and God was in reality less one of dependence than one of unparalleled intimacy.[28] Jesus trusted in and abandoned himself to God, as a child utterly trusts his father.[29] In return, the Father invested him with 'glory' when he gave him the Name, that is, the rank and dignity

---

[20]As in Acts 4:19; 7:52; 22:14.   [21]Is. 61:1, 42:1; cf. 45:1 ff.
[22]Acts 4:27; 10:38; cf. Luke 4:18.
[23]Acts 3:14; 4:27, 30; Mk. 1:24 and parallels; cf. Acts 2:27, 13:35 and Is. 43:14.
[24]Acts 3:18, 20; 4:10, 26; 2:36; 8:5; 9:22; 1 Cor. 15:3; Eph. 5:14.
[25]Cf. Acts 3:13, 26; 4:27, 30.   [26]Cf. Is. 42:1 ff; 49:3; 53:10-12.
[27]Cf. Is. 49:1 ff; 50:4 ff; 52:13-53:9.
[28]Cf. Acts 4:24-30 (for Jesus' intimacy with the Father).
[29]Cf. Phil. 2:6-8 and Acts 8:30-35.

of sovereign Lord and Saviour.[30] Immediately, then, the title 'Servant' began to take on more or less divine overtones. More precisely, it was seen as quite inseparable from the other titles 'Son' and 'Lord' (which it did in fact connote), and was thus at once the core and the richest expression of the primitive faith in Christ.

This can be seen in two texts. Philip's instruction of the Ethiopian (Acts 8 : 30-38) bears on the theme of 'Jesus the Servant' (v. 30-35), but it reaches a climax in the assertion that 'Jesus, the Christ, is the Son of God' (v. 37).[31] The hymn in Philippians 2 : 6-11 is even more precise : it shows that Christ, who is from all eternity the Son existing with the Father and now is divine Lord, thus fulfils completely the idea of the 'Servant', humiliated and glorified. This determines the true sense of the title 'Jesus the Servant'. What is more, it is evidence of the speed with which this theme developed in the first communities of Palestine.

'The Lord' (Psalm 110 : 1)

The earliest form of Christianity in Palestine laid stress on a further salient feature of the apostolic faith in Christ, the theme of 'the Lord Jesus'. The antecedents of this theme lie in Jewish belief in the Messiah-King, and in the pervasive influence of Psalm 110 : 1 on the teaching of Christ. And the theme stands in its own right as the first flowering of the paschal revelation of Jesus. Its great antiquity is indicated firstly by its link with the theme of 'Jesus the Servant', and by the use of the Aramaic formula *maranatha,* 'Come, Lord'

[30]Cf. Phil. 2:9-11 and Acts 2:12-26.
[31]Critical editions of *Acts* omit v. 37; the author, however, regards it as authentic. (The *Bible de Jérusalem* regards it as an ancient gloss. *Translator's note.*)

(or, 'The Lord is there')[32] and its Greek equivalent *Kyrios
Ièsous,* 'Jesus is Lord'.[33] This undoubtedly explains why it
dominated the thought and devotion of the apostolic Church
for so long.

But what meaning did it have?

The phrase 'Lord Jesus' held meanings of the utmost
complexity for the early Church; in fact it embraced all the
important themes which constituted the faith of the apostles.
In the first place it emphasized the fact that Jesus was the
Messiah-King and then, more precisely, the fact that Jesus
was God.

At the beginning, the notion of Messiah-King clearly
seemed to be dominant. The way in which the text of Psalm
110 (which from a very early date came to be the main
scriptural foundation for belief in Christ) is quoted in many
ancient texts points to this. On two occasions, it is mentioned
in connexion with Jesus' exaltation, i.e. his ascension to
heaven. The first of these is in Peter's address on the day of
Pentecost :

> It is this Jesus whom God has raised up, and of that we
> are all witnesses. Being therefore exalted to the right hand
> of God, and having received from the Father the promise
> of the Holy Spirit, he has poured out what you see and
> hear. For David did not ascend to heaven, but he did say :
> 'Jahweh said to my lord, sit at my right hand, until I make
> your enemies a stool under your feet'. Let all the house of
> Israel therefore know with certainty that God has made
> him both Lord and Christ, and this is the Jesus whom you
> have crucified (Acts 2 : 32-36; see also Ps. 110 : 1).

[32]See I Cor. 16:22.
[33]Apoc. 22:20; Acts 7:59; Phil. 2:11; I Cor. 12:3; Rom. 10:9;
cf. Acts 2:21, 36.

The same verse of Psalm 110 is repeated again when the apostles explained their new faith to the Sanhedrin :

> The God of our fathers raised Jesus whom you put to death by hanging him on a cross. God has raised him to his right hand as Leader and Saviour, to give Israel the power to repent and have forgiveness of sins (Acts 5 : 30-31).

Now in the apostolic communities, the exaltation of Christ was regarded precisely as the investiture, the enthronement of Christ as Messiah-King. According to the most primitive teaching found in Acts (chapters 1-10), Jesus, when 'seated at the right hand of God', 'received' the Spirit.[34] And it was under the influence and the impetus of the Spirit, that Jesus set up the Kingdom of God over whose destiny he will preside until the day of the Second Coming when his judgement will bring about its consummation.[35] This coupling from the very start of the Kingdom of God with the exaltation of Christ, of the Last Judgement and Parousia with the Ascension, leaves no doubt at all of the vital place which the theme of the Messiah-King played in the belief in the Lord Jesus.

But even in this earliest sense, the title 'Lord' did not indicate simply the possession of messianic dignity. In the eyes of the apostles, and even more in the eyes of their disciples, Jesus the Messiah-King was also transcendent and divine. By the very fact of his being 'exalted to the right hand' of the Father, Jesus possessed 'glory', 'power', 'dominion',[36] in other words the whole gamut of prerogatives and attributes hitherto reserved solely to Jahweh. Jesus, in a word, shared in the unique nature of the Father. There is no reason, of

[34]See Acts 2:32; compare 5:32 with 2:2-21.
[35]See Acts 10:42; cf. 3:19-21; 4:11-12; 2:40.
[36]See Acts 3:13; I Tim. 3:16; Rom. 1:4; Acts 2:16-21, 33; Phil. 2:10.

course, to suppose that the first Christians were fully aware of this fact from the very beginning. Yet the more they pondered the meaning of Psalm 110 in the light of the gospel revelation and their own experiences at Easter, and the more they weighed up the true value of their Master's newly won attributes, the nearer they came to an understanding, at once clearer and more penetrating, of the truth that Christ was God. From that moment the phrase 'Lord Jesus' became the standard expression of belief in Christ, true God. The ancient titles taken from Deuteronomy and Isaiah soon gave way before this new formula of faith which itself unhappily prevented, in some cases for many years, the acceptance of another definitive title, namely 'Jesus, Son of the Father'.

Christ Jesus in the life of his disciples

As a final consideration, there is a basic *religious fact* which shows how quickly the Church arrived at a full awareness of the mystery of Christ.

In the prayer of the Jerusalem Church (Acts 4 : 24-30), the 'Servant' Jesus is still regarded as the instrument of the 'Lord' God in the work of salvation. But Peter's discourse in the Temple (3:12-26) and even more Acts chapter 2 show that it is the Lord Christ who, in the salvation of both individual and community, exercises the prerogatives previously ascribed to Jahweh. This progress in faith doubtless showed itself in preaching before it came to affect prayer; doubtless also, it may have appeared rather earlier among the hellenists, always more sensitive to the great messianic themes of the Old Testament and the Gospel. But it is none the less true that it made a deep impression, and that at a very early date, on the whole religious life of Palestinian Christianity.

Henceforth, Jesus, the Lord of the Church, is seen to be the perfect accomplishment of the theocratic order, and therefore also of the economy of salvation. He purifies the Church through baptism, he sanctifies it by the Spirit; he brings it to perfection in himself, the 'Just One'; and as Judge he avenges any violation of its sanctity. At the level of the individual, to him is directed obedience by faith, praise in the liturgy, and the proclamation of the great deeds of God. The life of the just man was once dominated by the ideal of the imitation of God; now, the life of a disciple is governed by the law of the imitation of Christ. The death of Stephen, faithful reproduction of the 'martyrdom' of Jesus, is significant from this point of view :[37] it expresses the fullness of the early Church's faith in Christ who is God.

[37]Cf. Acts 7:59 compared with Luke 23:46; Acts 7:55 compared with Mark 14:62 and parallels.

The Divinity of Christ in the Synoptic Gospels

P. Benoit, O.P.

III

The Divinity of Christ in the Synoptic Gospels

P. Benoit O.P.

The Value of the Synoptic Tradition

THERE IS NO doubt that the authors of the first three gospels believed in Jesus' divinity. Matthew and Luke not only give an account of his miraculous conception, which they ascribe to the direct influence of the Holy Spirit,[1] but in addition all three very frequently repeat the title 'Son of God', sometimes in conjunction with the name Christ.[2] Occasionally indeed they make a distinction between them,[3] as though to make it quite clear that they regard the former as something more than an ordinary messianic title. Even Mark who, in the form in which we have the gospels, can be regarded as the oldest of them, already shares this belief. At one time scholars endeavoured to discover in his gospel Christian belief in its most primitive form, not yet contaminated by what they claimed was Pauline speculation; at this stage, they held, Jesus was looked on not as the incarnate Son of God but merely as a Wise Man, a Prophet or, at the most, as Messiah. This hypothesis could not stand up to the facts, and scholars have now been forced to recognize that the second gospel already contains in essence the belief in Jesus, Son of God, which later witnesses of revelation would continue to make more explicit. A contemporary exegete can sum up his own opinion and that of many others on this point in these words : 'The christology of Mark is as lofty as any other in

[1] Matt. 1:18-20; Lk. 1:31-35.   [2] Mk. 1:1; Matt. 16:16.
[3] Lk. 22:67-70.

the New Testament, not excluding John's.'[4] It is sufficient to
note that the synoptic gospels were written at a time when
belief in the divinity of Jesus was clearly expressed in
Christian circles, particularly by Paul, whose great letters are
of an earlier date than the composition of the second gospel.
In view of the strictly divine significance that Paul gives to
the title 'Son of God', it is unthinkable that Mark, his disciple, much under his influence, would mean something else
when he used the same term in his own gospel. This is true,
a fortiori, for Matthew and Luke.

But this is precisely where the difficulty arises. When the
synoptic writers proclaimed the divinity of Jesus, they might
conceivably have projected upon the Saviour's human life
the light of a belief which was only a much later development. This light may not have distorted the historical facts
of Jesus' life, but it may have given them a significance which
they did not have originally. The time is past when the
authors of the Gospels could be regarded as frauds who
deliberately mutilated the real facts in order to use them for
their own propaganda. Their faith is too artless to allow of
any such suggestion and most modern critics have recognized
this fact. But might it be a case of well-intentioned, unconscious remoulding of Jesus' actions and attitudes, resulting
from the belief in his Person which grew up after his death
and, in particular, from his resurrection? This raises a
serious problem and demands honest consideration.

Our faith has the right to rely on the faith of the evangelists, on the testimony of the inspired authors who bring us
the Word of God; but our reason likewise has the right to
examine their testimony and its value as history, so that
through it we can grasp what Jesus did in fact do and say.
If we can discover the mind of Jesus himself, if we can see

[4]Vincent Taylor, *The Gospel According to St Mark*, p. 121
(Macmillan, London, 1952).

the way in which he conceived his own person and mission, this will be our best guarantee that his disciples remained faithful to his intentions and have not distorted his image. This procedure, which is the prerogative of every believer, becomes an absolute essential when one comes to scrutinize the ideas of scholars who do not share the faith, and who deny any value as inspired writings to the texts, allowing them only the value of human testimony.

Happily, even if we do treat the gospels merely as human testimony, we are still on firm ground. Honest study of the synoptic gospels has brought critics more and more to recognize the sober authenticity of the words and deeds they attribute to Jesus. It is true that even in recent years some critics have shown a tendency to treat the greater part of the gospel material as a creation of the primitive Christian community and have thus rejected the possibility of knowing what Jesus really said or did. But such radical scepticism is becoming more rare. The preaching of the primitive community in its various forms of kerygma, catechesis, exhortation and apologetic discussion certainly exercised a considerable influence on the pericopes collected in our gospels; this is a new and fruitful point of view to which modern exegesis owes its best discoveries. Yet it seems clear that such influence was exerted more over the form than over the content, more over the literary presentation of the facts than over the substance of the facts themselves. The actual needs of preaching unquestionably governed the choice of the reminiscences of Jesus which alone, from among so many others, were chosen, and the interests which directed the choice of these also directed their literary form, as theology rather than biography, and their arrangement, which was logical rather than chronological. Preoccupations of this kind, however, do not seem to have led to the distortion of the disciples' reminiscences of Jesus, and there is no reason

why we should regard them as fabrications invented after
the event. The earliest witnesses were clearly anxious to base
their faith and preaching on reliable and honestly reported
facts; and this evident concern makes it impossible to attribute to them too easily the creation, albeit unconscious, of
an entire legend, as some critics imagine. While it is true
that, when they wrote of Jesus, they had no intention of
writing *history* in the strict sense of the word, it is equally
true that their intention was to record only what was
historical.

The best proof of this may be seen in the sober tone and
archaic atmosphere of the synoptic gospels. Though they
were written some thirty or forty years after the death of
Jesus, at a time when the theology of Paul and probably that
of John were already flourishing, the memories of Jesus
which they report are characterized by an unadorned sim-
plicity which is very true to life. They are as yet untouched
by the speculative theology of John and Paul, or by the
unbridled quest for the sensational so characteristic of the
apocryphal gospels. They reproduce sayings which are
semitic in form and content, such as Jesus must have spoken.
They continue to put into his mouth archaic expressions such
as 'Son of Man' which later theology did not take into its
vocabulary. They even preserve sayings which a more highly
developed Christianity found embarrassing, such as the admission of ignorance by the Son, the proclamation of an
imminent Parousia, and the assurance that not one iota of
the Law would be disregarded. The impression they give
(except in a few unessential details, particularly in Matthew)
is of a faithful and punctilious attachment to a tradition
dating from Jesus' own time, long before their present edited
form. Had the Synoptists intended to apply to the person of
Jesus the theology of Incarnation and Redemption in the
form in which it was being developed at the time they were

writing they would have expressed themselves in a very different way. There is no doubt that they already present Jesus as the Son of God who came to bring salvation to men through his redeeming death. They express these ideas, however, in an archaic and rudimentary form which does not derive from the theology of John and Paul—on the contrary, it forms the basis of their theology—and must have its source in Jesus himself. Modern criticism has now fortunately turned back to this view. It has ceased to ascribe the essential message of Christianity to the brilliance of Paul and later John, and has come to the conclusion that the true author could only have been Jesus.

The precise topic we are concerned with at the moment is that of Christ's divinity, and in our consideration of it we can now examine the synoptic evidence, secure in the knowledge that their primitive character guarantees that they are a genuine record of what Jesus claimed to be and what he did to prove it.

The Argument from Miracles

Jesus was never satisfied with words alone; his word was always backed by deeds. This he had to do to justify his unusual claims and the unconditional adherence to his person which he demanded. The most cursory reading of the Gospels makes us feel what crucial significance his wonderful deeds had for those who believed in him. It was because he demonstrated supreme power over nature, and particularly over sick or dead bodies and evil spirits that his disciples saw in him the absolutely unique being he claimed to be. So before we examine what Jesus claimed to be, it would be well to evaluate the importance of the deeds he performed to support his claims.

Miracles are not in themselves a proof of the divinity of the one who performs them. Every age has known its human

wonder-workers, and in the time of Jesus himself the belief
was widespread that there were men endowed with divine
powers which allowed them to act on nature in defiance of
its ordinary laws. This fact must be borne well in mind so as
not to over-estimate the importance of the argument from
miracles, but to gain a true understanding of its place in the
context of the gospel.

The rabbinical writings frequently record instances of
miracle-working rabbis. Some, for example, healed incurable
diseases, others made the dumb speak, even raised the dead,
calmed storms and induced rain to fall. Mention was also
made of special types of healers like Rabbi Hanina ben
Dosa, around whom was woven a strange legend of fabulous
deeds, each one more astounding than its predecessor. In the
Greek world, likewise, belief in extraordinary events and
miraculous cures was very widely held. Sometimes the
miracles are the work of gods like Aesculapius of Epidaurus
or Serapis of Canopus, whose amazing cures are remem-
bered in literature and recorded on inscriptions; sometimes
they are the work of men, 'wise' men like Pythagoras and
Apollonius of Tyana whose more or less romanticized lives
meticulously retail their superhuman activities. The prophets of the Old Testament, for example Elias and Eliseus,
also worked wonders. They made fire fall from heaven,[5]
made the rain to fall,[6] sweetened brackish water,[7] created
an unfailing supply of bread and oil,[8] and raised the dead to
life.[9] Moses, the greatest prophet of them all, was renowned
for the wonders he did during the flight from Egypt. From
the Messiah, therefore, not less was expected—though it was

[5] 1 Kings 18:21-40; 2 Kings 1:9-14.
[6] 1 Kings 18:41-46.   [7] 2 Kings 2:19-22.
[8] 1 Kings 17:7-16; 2 Kings 4:1-7, 42-44.
[9] 1 Kings 17:24; 2 Kings 18:37.

not unduly stressed nor considered exclusive to him, this power shared by so many others.

At first sight, therefore, it would seem that the miracles in the gospel put Jesus no higher than the many wonder-workers found at that time in the Jewish and Greek worlds. But underlying this superficial similarity there is a profound difference, which is apparent as soon as we scrutinize more closely the way in which he performed his miracles and the significance he claimed to give them.

In the first place Jesus' miracles differ from those of his contemporaries by their credibility and, if one may use the word, their naturalness. The miracles of the Rabbis or of Epidaurus are mounted on an accumulation of improbabilities; for example, there is the Rabbi who struck dead one of his colleagues when he thought he saw a jeering smile on his face, and finding he had been mistaken, promptly raised him to life again;[10] or take Aesculapius, who delivered a woman, after a five-year pregnancy, of a child which as soon as it was born began to walk and play as though it were five years old.[11] By contrast with these stories, the miracles of healing in the gospels seem to be singularly credible; and while some can be explained by psychological influence, which is better appreciated nowadays, most of them demand the intervention of a supernatural power, which can only be denied by a prejudice based on philosophical principles.

Jesus exercised this power with a magisterial authority, and this is another characteristic distinguishing his activities from those of contemporary healers. Rabbis performed miracles only after a long period of prayer which they admitted was frequently in vain.[12] Aesculapius acted through

[10]*Babylonian Talmud,* BQ 117ab.
[11]Dittenberger, *Syll. Inscriptiones Graecae,* (ed. 3), vol. III, no. 1168, 1 ff.
[12]*Babylonian Talmud,* Taan, 23 ab; Ber. 34b

dreams : sometimes he performed surgical operations which
were absolutely incredible, not to say grotesque (a case of
dropsy was cured by cutting the patient's head off, tipping
him upside down to let the water run out, and then sticking
the head on again);[13] or else he simply recommended a more
or less hygienic treatment which the priests of the sanctuary
of Epidaurus obviously borrowed from the medical ideas
current at the time.[14] Jesus acted on his own authority,
using a simple gesture or more commonly a word—a word
which was immediately followed by its effect.[15] The only
serious comparison which could be made would be with
Pythagoras or Apollonius of Tyana; similar cures are described in their lives, but these were written after the gospels
and can reasonably be suspected of plagiarism in the interests of religious controversy.

The sobriety and even restraint which Jesus showed with
regard to his miracles is another characteristic which makes
him stand out from the wonder-workers of his time.
Rabbinic legends and hellenistic tales amass marvellous
deeds at will; but the gospel shows us how reserved Jesus was
in this matter. He rarely took the initiative; on the contrary
he acted almost as if with reluctance, moved by the misery or
the faith of those who importuned him; he gave instructions
that the miracles he had agreed to perform should not be
publicized;[16] and when he failed to discern in a petitioner
the dispositions necessary to make a demonstration of his
power effective, he refused or, as the gospel forthrightly puts
it, he found himself unable to act at all.[17] He knew only too
well the delight the people of his time took in marvels, which

[13]See Dittenberger, op. cit., vol. I, no. 1169, 1 ff.
[14]Dittenberger, op. cit., vol. I, no. 1170.
[15]Mk. 1:31; 1:41 ff; 2:11 ff; 3:5; 4:39 etc. and parallel passages.
[16]Mk. 1:44; 5:43; 7:36 etc.
[17]Mk. 6:5 and Matt. 13:58

fed a curiosity which was childish and lacked the power to convert the soul. Jesus advised his disciples, who were somewhat naïvely exulting in the power he had given them, to rejoice rather that their names had been written in heaven.[18]

It was always for a higher reason that Jesus consented to work wonders and occasionally took the initiative in doing them : namely, to give authority to his mission, to win faith in his Word. There was nothing of the sort with the rabbis, for whom a miracle was merely a manifestation of divine power, whose human intermediary was not important and deserved little interest. To them a teacher merited greater respect than a wonder-worker.[19] The same can be said of the miracles of Epidaurus : the power of Aesculapius was not the point at issue; the wonderful cures related with such gusto were intended only to uphold the reputation of the sanctuary. We have already commented on the place of Pythagoras and Apollonius of Tyana, the last challenge that a dying paganism held up to the conquering figure of Christ. When Jesus performed his miracles, it was as a 'sign', to stimulate the mind to see in them something more than just another marvel. Faith was the pre-requisite he demanded or to which he bowed;[20] not merely faith in God the Lord of nature—at that time and in that world this was never called in doubt—but faith in *his* person, as one whose mission God was accredited in this way. Which brings us back, then, to the question of what Jesus claimed to be when he supported his message with signs like these. Miracles, if authentic, prove precisely what they are asked to prove. Did Jesus work miracles to make men accept him merely as a wonder-worker in possession of unusual powers? Was it to reveal

[18]Lk. 10:20.   [19]*Babylonian Talmud,* Ber. 34b.
[20]Mk. 2:5; 5:34; 9:23 ff; Matt. 8:10-13; 9:28; Lk. 17:19.

himself as the Messiah? Or was it to suggest something
deeper?

Jesus 'the Messiah'

There is no need for us to demonstrate at length that
Jesus did not present himself only as a rabbi amongst many
others, a teacher and a wonder-worker. We have already
noticed that the authoritative way in which he performed
his miracles was fundamentally different from that of the
rabbis for whom miracles were the answer to humble and
laborious prayer. And as for being merely a teaching rabbi,
his whole manner of teaching was opposed to that of the
rabbis who kept scrupulously to the tradition of the ancients,
only venturing a personal opinion to solve disputed cases:
'he taught them as one who had authority, and not as their
Scribes'.[21]

Jesus treated the Law and Tradition as though he were
their master, interpreting, deepening and even correcting
them. He claimed the right to transgress the Sabbath when
that served better to fulfil the loving intentions of the divine
will.[22] In place of a still imperfect morality which dealt
only with material actions, he substituted demands which
penetrated even to the heart: 'You have heard that it was
said to the men of old . . . but I say to you'.[23] To the relaxa-
tions of the marriage bond granted by Moses himself because
of human weakness, he opposed the absoluteness of the holy
will of God which forbade even divorce.[24] He claimed indeed to uphold the law, but to do so by interpreting it in a
new spirit which fulfilled and transformed it. His mission was
to bring new wine, which he refused to spoil by compromise,

[21]Matt. 7:29.
[22]Mk. 2:23-28; 3:1-5 and parallels. Lk. 13:10-17; 14:1-6.
[23]Matt. 5:21-48.   [24]Mk. 10:2-12 and Matt. 19:1-9.

by putting it as he said 'into old wine-skins';[25] he was beginning a new age, the age of the Kingdom of God, heralded for
so long by the prophets and now inaugurated in his own
Person.[26] When he drove out unclean spirits, he was des-
troying the kingdom of Satan and setting up the Kingdom
of God through the Holy Spirit.[27] His miracles brought to
pass what the prophets, and Isaiah in particular, had proclaimed; they accompanied and clearly indicated the coming of the Messianic age.[28]

We must, therefore, admit at least that Jesus professed
to be the Messiah. After a certain period of doubt, there is
now growing unanimity among exegetes on this subject.
Jesus' messianism could hardly have been a complete invention of the disciples, after their Master's death and contrary to his intentions. Such an invention, completely
unsupported by any statement of Jesus himself, is in itself
highly unlikely; and in addition the details handed on by the
gospel tradition are too certain, and point too clearly in the
one direction, for us to be able to dismiss them all as posthu-
mous creations of prejudiced apologists. Jesus claimed that
in his own person and with sovereign power the messianic
age of the Kingdom of God was inaugurated : this constitutes
the very substance of the gospel; to reject this claim one
must as well reject the gospel in its entirety.

We must conclude that Jesus presented himself as the
Messiah. But this does not necessarily involve us in a confession of his divinity. The Messiah awaited by the leaders
of official religious thought in Judaism was a man, a King
of David's lineage, endowed by God with extraordinary
powers, one who would gain victory after victory, but

[25]Mk. 2:22 and parallels.
[26]Mk. 2:19; 4; Matt. 12:28; 12:41 f; 13:16 f; Lk. 17:21.
[27]Mk. 3:23-27 and parallels; Lk. 10:18.
[28]Matt. 11:2-6 and Lk. 7:18-23.

nonetheless always simply a man, with nothing of the divine
in his make-up. All the claims of Jesus that we have noted so
far, namely his supreme authority over the Law, his inauguration of the Kingdom of God, his miraculous command of
nature, his insistence on unconditional faith in himself and
his mission, all these could surely be explained as the
claims of a human, not a divine, Messiah. The crowds and
the suppliants who hailed him with the title 'Son of
David'[29] surely saw nothing more in him; and we may
not unreasonably think that for a long time the disciples
themselves went no further than this messianic faith.
Peter's confession at Caesarea, as reported by Mark and
Luke, does not imply anything more;[30] and the rest of
the passage shows that even this faith was far from
perfect.[31]

Yet, little by little, they did ascend to faith in the divinity
of their Master. The miracle of the Resurrection was on its
own hardly sufficient to bring about such a complete upheaval; it must have been prepared for by the words and
deeds of Jesus himself.

We do, in fact, find in the gospel clear pointers to the
conclusion that Jesus' claims were on an altogether higher
level than ordinary messianism. On the one hand he put
forward the notion of a spiritual and moral Kingdom of
God, planted gently and growing slowly,[32] in opposition to
the materialistic dreams of a conquering, political messianism; and on the other hand he claimed for himself powers
and titles which exceeded those traditionally attributed to
the Messiah.

[29]Mk. 10:47 ff. and parallels; Matt. 9:27; 12:23; 15:22; 21:9
and 15.
[30]Mk. 8:27-30 and Lk. 9:18-21.   [31]Mk. 9:31-33.
[32]See the parables of the Kingdom in Mark 4 and Matthew
passim.

In the first place, he laid claim to the power of forgiving sin,[33] a power which had never been recognized as messianic but had always been reserved jealously to God himself, as is shown by the reaction of the scribes on this occasion.[34] Now it is most unlikely that such an exorbitant claim could be the creation of the first Christians, attributed by them to Jesus. He alone would have had the audacity to make such a claim; and in so doing, he was laying claim to a divine attribute— and this could only lead to a further conclusion, or else be rejected as blasphemy.

Moreover, there are in the synoptists two titles used in reference to Jesus which could surpass those of the Messiah of tradition and which, therefore, demand a closer examination. They are the titles *Son of God* and *Son of Man*.

Jesus 'Son of God'

At first sight it may appear that the first of these titles is the stronger and more unambiguous, sufficient of itself to settle the question. If Jesus really called himself the 'Son of God', or allowed himself to be called that, there need be no more discussion—the synoptists have assured us of his divinity and the matter is ended. However, the problem is more complicated than that, because the title did not always possess the precise, transcendental significance it has acquired for our faith under the influence of the New Testament writings and through the theological reflection which formulated the faith of those writings.

'Son of God' means for us the ontological sonship of someone who possesses the divine nature because of his eternal generation from the Father. Before it reached this stage of precision, however, the doctrine had a long history, during which the sonship it refers to was understood in the very

---

[33]Mk. 2:10 and parallels.   [34]Mk. 2:7.

much looser sense of a sonship in the moral, not the metaphysical, order of reality. We have only to open the Bible to
see how true this is. The angels are frequently called 'sons of
God',[35] and this cannot possibly mean a share in God's
nature—something particularly obnoxious to Hebrew
monotheism—but rather a special intimacy between the
heavenly beings and the God whose 'court' they constitute.
Elsewhere the expression is used of men. Jahweh called Israel
his 'first born son',[36] he looked on him as a son,[37] and the
Egyptians admitted that he was a 'son of God'.[38] This is
evidently a matter of a moral, adoptive sonship,[39] the effect
of the loving choice[40] by which God singled out his people,[41]
a choice they were required to live up to by behaving as
sons.[42] The honour of being 'sons of God' bestowed on the
Chosen People as a body obviously applied to the individuals
who made up this people : 'You are the sons of Jahweh your
God';[43] 'they will be called sons of the living God'.[44] And if
in addition to sharing the common election, there were some
personal grounds of special intimacy with God, then the
title 'son of God' could be used with even greater force. This
intimacy might take the form of piety; for example to show
kindness to orphans was to behave like 'a son of the Most
High';[45] the righteous man, too, who knows God and keeps
his Law 'gives himself out as the son of God ... boasts that
he has God for his Father'.[46] Alternatively, the title might
refer to an individual's standing in society. Princes and

---

[35]Ps. 29:1; 39:7; Job 1:6; 2:1; 38:7.
[36]Exod. 4:22.   [37]Deut. 1:31; 8:5; Hosea 11:1.
[38]Wis. 18:13.   [39]Jerem. 3:19.
[40]Jer. 31:20.   [41]Deut. 32:6 ff; Ecclus. 36:14.
[42]Jerem. 3:19; Mal. 1:6.   [43]Deut. 14:1.
[44]Hosea 1:10. See also Is. 1:2, 4; 30:1, 9; 43:6; Prov. 3:12; Ps.
103:13; Judith 9:4; Esther 16:16; Wis. 9:7; 12:19-21; 16:10.
[45]Ecclus. 4:10.   [46]Wisdom 2:13, 16; cf. 5:5.

judges were 'gods' or 'sons of the Most High'.[47] And above all, it was the King, anointed by Jahweh, the representative of his people, who deserved to be thought of as the son of God in preference to all others. This idea was extremely widespread in the ancient world, where the people were accustomed to seeing something divine in kingship. The monotheism of the Bible adapted itself to this universally held belief and looked on the King as becoming an adopted son of God by virtue of his election. Thus, Jahweh says of the heir he promised David through the prophet Nathan : 'I shall be a father to him, and he shall be a son to me'.[48] And since this same prophecy included also a promise that David's dynasty would last for ever, this filial adoption clearly applies in advance to all the descendants of David down to the greatest of them, the Messiah. The Messiah-King is actually addressed by Jahweh in Psalm 2 thus: 'You are my son, today (the day of your accession) I have begotten you'--a phrase echoed and commented upon in Psalm 89: 'He shall cry to me, "You are my father, my God, and the rock of my salvation". And I make him the first born, the highest of the kings of the earth.'

The title 'Son of God' did not in fact become an attribute characteristic of the Messiah, as has sometimes been claimed. It belonged simply to a different context of ideas, both wider and more precise than a messianic context : wider, because it could apply to others than the Messiah; more precise because it denotes the specific quality of special intimacy with God, whether this be in the Messiah or in others. The title itself does not indicate the source of this intimacy : it could be a relationship of service, or of knowledge, or of loving obedience, or, finally, of nature.

[47]Ps. 82:6; cf. 58:1.
[48]2 Sam. 7:14; 1 Chron. 17:13; 22:10; 28:6.

It is evident that we must take account of this literary tradition in the Bible, if we are to appreciate the term 'Son of God' when it occurs in the gospel. Some scholars would rather search for the key to its meaning in other Eastern religions or in the Greco-Roman culture, but they do so only by sacrificing the authenticity of the gospel tradition, taking it as the creation of the hellenistic Christian communities. This could never be admitted unless and until it has been shown that every explanation in terms of a semitic and Palestinian background is out of the question, which certainly has not happened in this case. What we have just seen of the Old Testament background makes it abundantly clear that the Jews in Palestine could call Jesus 'the son of God', and that he also could use it to refer to himself. We must consider the sense in which they used it. The idea of a natural sonship would definitely not be the first to come to the minds of Jesus' contemporaries; we may even say that it would be the most difficult for them, the most repugnant to the jealous monotheism of Jewish thought. The term was susceptible of such a transcendental meaning, and one day it would receive this meaning, at the end of a long evolution. We have seen that this was to be the case with the evangelists, when they came to compose their works with a faith at last fully enlightened. But at the moment, we are concerned with what significance the expression could have had for Jesus and his contemporaries.

The unclean spirits who bestowed the title 'Son of God' upon Jesus through the mouths of people possessed might have recognized him only as the Messiah but, on the other hand, they might have guessed more.[49] Whether they did so or not is extremely difficult to say, but at least the bystanders were surely unable to see in the name anything

[49]Mk. 3:11; 5:7 and parallels.

more than a messianic attribute. Luke assumes this: 'and demons also came out of many crying "You are the Son of God". But he rebuked them, and would not allow them to speak, *because they knew that he was the Christ'*(Lk. 4:41 ff). When Satan said to Jesus during the temptation in the desert, 'if you are the Son of God'[50] he seems to be referring to the voice from heaven which was heard when God manifested himself at Christ's baptism.[51] This saying was itself a combination of two prophetic utterances of the old Testament, about the Messiah and the Servant of Jahweh respectively, neither of which necessarily implied the notion of a natural sonship in the metaphysical order. They could, of course, be extended to this latter meaning and, as we shall see, a transcendental significance is the one which best suits Jesus' inner-consciousness, but it is doubtful whether Satan possessed a clear view of this mystery from the beginning. His questions, and his attempt to lead into evil someone who appeared to him as no more than a dangerous rival, seem to indicate his ignorance. At all events the disciples did not reach such an exalted conclusion, at least not at the beginning of their training. They needed time to appreciate even the fact that Jesus was the Messiah. And the very human way in which even then they interpreted his messianic role,[52] the dullness of heart for which Jesus so often rebuked them,[53] their scandal at the crucifixion,[54] all of this makes it impossible to believe that they had any clear awareness of their master's divinity before their eyes were opened—and even then with difficulty—by the great miracle of the Resurrection.[55] Matthew has recorded two

---

[50]Matt. 4:3, 6; Lk. 4:3, 9.   [51]Mk. 1:11; Matt. 3:17; Lk. 3:22.
[52]Matt. 16:23; Mk. 8:33.
[53]Mk. 4:13, 40; 7:18; 8:17 f, 21; 9:19; 10:38. See also 6:52; 9:32.
[54]Mk. 14:27, 30, 50, 66-72 and parallels; Lk. 22:31-34; 24:21.
[55]Matt. 28:17; Lk. 24:25, 41.

episodes in which the disciples came to recognize Jesus as
the 'Son of God' and in context they go beyond the simple
idea of messianic dignity. Peter found it inadequate to confess 'you are the Christ', and added 'Son of the living God'
(Matt. 16 : 16); and before that, in 14 : 33, after the miracle
of the walking on the sea, the disciples to a man, over-
whelmed by this manifestation of the supernatural, prost-
rated themselves and cried: 'Truly you are the Son of God'.
The parallel passages in Mark,[56] however, make no mention
of these protestations, and since we can hardly imagine that
he chose to omit assertions of such significance altogether, we
may ask ourselves whether Matthew (which in its Greek form
is certainly later than Mark) has not added them under the
influence of a more highly developed faith. As for the cry
of the centurion at the foot of the cross,[57] no one will look for
a formal confession of Christ's divinity, in the sense that we
understand it, from a pagan : if his words have been reported
accurately (although Luke[58] writes : 'Surely this was a just
man'), they are quite adequately explained as a reference to
the contemptuous accusations made by the Jewish leaders
in his hearing.[59] These accusations themselves are the
significant thing here; since they are based on claims which
Jesus made throughout his ministry and particularly before
the Sanhedrin, they must be weighed in all their seriousness.
We had to recognize that during the life of Jesus neither men
nor demons were able to penetrate the mystery of his divinity;
but we must now admit that Jesus himself was fully aware
of it and spoke of it in a way which was necessarily enigmatic,
but which suggested enough to prompt questions about his
real nature, and enough to form the basis of a belief which
would blossom into maturity after his victory over death.

[56]Mk. 8:29; 6:51 f.   [57]Mk. 15:39; Matt. 27:54.
[58]Lk. 23:47.   [59]Matt. 27:40 and 43.

Jesus never said outright : 'I am the Son of God.' It was something he simply could not say at a time when a statement of this kind could never be understood in its true sense. But he did better. He revealed a union between himself and God his Father so singular and transcendent that it had the effect of placing him on the same divine level as the Father. This is the force of those statements in which he claimed to be not only a son but 'the Son'. There is a striking significance in the allusion, discreetly inserted in the parable of the unfaithful vine-dressers, to himself, the only son, the heir,[60] sent by the Father after his servants the prophets. And for those who still refuse to see in this any more than a possible title of the Messiah, we need only refer to other sayings whose authenticity is no less assured, which plumb the depths of the intimate relationship suggested by this title.

One of the most famous sayings, famous for good reason, is the 'Confiteor tibi Pater' which reveals the union of knowledge and love between Christ and his Father : 'All things have been delivered to me by my Father; and no one knows the Son except the Father, and no one knows the Father except the Son and anyone to whom the Son chooses to reveal him.'[61] This astonishing statement, which belongs to one of the most ancient sources of the synoptic tradition, casts a singularly revealing light on Jesus' consciousness of the unique relationship he bore to God. He knows him immediately and completely; this knowledge lays bare to him all the Father's secrets, and makes him the only means by which these secrets can be manifested to men. There is an unmistakable Joannine ring about the saying, which has prompted some scholars to cast suspicion on its authenticity. But there is nothing to justify such suspicion; on the contrary, it is an extremely important support for all those

[61]Matt. 11:27 and Lk. 10:22.   [60]Mk. 12:6 and parallels.

affirmations in the fourth gospel which some scholars are too inclined to reject out of hand as reflecting later theology. John has certainly marked his work with the strong imprint of his genius and has set down the Lord's teaching with all the skill of his powerful contemplative mind. But there is room also to think that he alone has conserved a whole aspect of the teaching of Jesus, an aspect which, being of less interest for ordinary catechetical needs, never found a place in the small pericopes of current preaching of which the synoptists were composed.

Moreover, there are other passages in the synoptic gospels which give further support to our claim that Jesus was aware of a unique relationship between himself and his Father. The first is his custom of contrasting 'my Father' with 'your Father' in order to draw a clear distinction between himself and his disciples. Yet the God of heaven was their Father too,[62] they were 'sons of God'[63] in the wide, moral sense in which all the Israelites were. But Jesus never put himself on the same level as them in this matter of sonship;[64] he never says 'our Father' (Matt. 6:9, the only place where this phrase occurs, obviously refers only to Christians, in whose mouth Jesus puts this prayer); he says rather 'my Father',[65] indicating thus that the relationship between himself and God is of a special kind, one which befits the 'beloved' Son,[66] that is to say, the only Son.

There is another saying of importance in this context, where Jesus calls himself the 'Son', while at the same time

---

[62]Matt. 5:45; cf. 5:16, 48; 6:1-6 etc; 7:11; 10:20; etc; Mk. 11:25; Lk. 6:35 ff; 12:30, 32; 22:29; 24:49.   [63]Matt. 5:9; Lk. 20:36.

[64]Matt. 17:26 is an exception; here he deigns to associate in his privilege of exemption from taxation those who were his brothers because they obeyed his Father; cf. Matt. 12:50.

[65]Matt. 7:21; 10:32-33; 11:27; 12:50; etc. Lk. 2:49; 10:22; 22:29; 24:49.

[66]Mk. 1:11; 9:7 and parallels; 12:6; Lk. 20:13; Matt. 12:18.

saying that the time of the Day of Judgement is unknown to him.[67] An admission of this sort would seriously offend more developed theological ideas—Luke makes no mention of it at all and some manuscripts of Matthew omit the words 'nor the Son'—and this only gives a greater guarantee of its authenticity. But, while admitting his ignorance, Jesus clearly ranges himself above the angels: 'But of that day and hour no one knows, not even the angels of heaven, nor the Son, but the Father only'; and in so doing he boldly ranks himself immediately next to God, a claim which is not affected even by his confession of ignorance. He whom the Father had given full knowledge of all mysteries could admit his ignorance of something which did not immediately concern his mission.[68] This clear statement, no matter how we explain it, obliges us to take seriously the humility of the Incarnation; it casts a precious ray of light on the relationship of the Father and the Son, a relationship which does in fact imply a certain subordination, hinted at in other texts of the synoptists themselves;[69] but this subordination is not in the order of being but in the order of function and in no way prevents the Son sharing in the Father's divine nature. The best proof of this is to be found in St Paul; for him the divinity of our Lord is never in doubt, yet he continually maintains the subordination of the Son to the Father in the economy of redemption; for example, it was the Father who raised the Son to life, and it will be the Son at the end of time who will hand over his kingdom to the Father and be subject to him.[70] And after Paul, the whole of primitive Christian theology calls Jesus 'Son of God', rather than 'God'—this name remained in a certain sense reserved to the Father.

[67]Mk. 13:32 and Matt. 24:36.   [68]Matt. 11:27.
[69]Mk. 10:40 and Matt. 20:23; Mk. 10:17 and parallels; Matt. 12:32 and Lk. 12:10.
[70]1 Thess. 1:10; 1 Cor. 15:24-28.

When Jesus called himself the Son, then, he was expressing, in a way that was veiled but still quite clear, his awareness of an exceptional intimacy with God which far exceeded
the legitimate claim of any man; and his hearers too were
well aware of it. The Jews were horrified. And the disciples,
when their faith was fully enlightened by the resurrection
and the gift of the Spirit, realized that their master could
only have used such words because he belonged to the divine
world. Nevertheless, for all that, it would be possible to cling
to the view that these statements of Jesus do not inevitably
indicate his divinity, that they could be the result of a highly
developed messianic consciousness; we have already seen
how even the human Messiah could be referred to as 'Son of
God'. However extraordinary the intimacy Jesus claimed
with the Father, it could conceivably be explained as a metaphor, sonship in the moral sense. Alternatively, the title might
be considered as anticipatory; if we must say that Jesus belonged to the divine order, it would be because he was somehow adopted into it by the glorification which followed his
death—not because he had already existed as divine. To
answer this difficulty, we must now move on to consider the
significance of the second title, namely 'Son of Man'. Para-
doxical as it may seem, this apparently humble title gives us
an even deeper insight into his intimate, inner consciousness
than the title 'Son of God'.

Jesus 'Son of Man'

This mysterious title has given rise to the most divergent
interpretations, and there are even critics who claim that
Jesus never applied it to himself. Their view is that it was
created by the earliest Christian communities as a way of
referring to Jesus, and was only later put into his mouth.
This hypothesis, however, runs completely counter not only
to the date of the gospel, but to the date of the whole of the

New Testament. Had the title really been an invention of the earliest Christians and the result of their desire to express the individuality of their Master, it would surely be found among their theological writings, for example, in Paul's letters. But in fact there is no trace of it there, and hardly a trace of it outside the gospels; the only exceptions are Acts 7 :56, where Stephen is clearly referring to Jesus' words before the Sanhedrin,[71] and the Apocalypse,[72] where the identification of the glorious Messiah with the Son of Man is presumed, rather than expressed, by the use of imagery from the book of Daniel.[73] It is only in the gospels that this title appears as a common expression, and always in the mouth of Jesus himself (the crowd's question in John 12 :34 is only a repetition of Jesus' own words of 12 :23-32). The impression we are given is that this was one of his favourite ways of referring to himself, and the fact that one or other of the synoptists occasionally writes 'me' instead of 'Son of Man' only confirms this impression.[74] Most contemporary scholars would agree that Jesus was the first, we may say the only one, to distinguish himself in this way. But certain scholars have attempted to explain the title in a very anaemic sense, by suggesting that its Aramaic equivalent means no more than simply 'the man'. This is not quite correct; Aramaic possesses other, simpler expressions to convey this idea. The phrase 'son of man' is unusual in Aramaic, and is normally used only in the plural to denote the members of the human race.[75] If it was unusual in Aramaic, it was even more unusual when translated into Greek, which probably explains why the authors of the New Testament, who wrote in Greek, did not adopt it. The fathers of the Church

[74]Compare Matt. 16:13 with Mk. 8:27 and Lk. 9:18; Mk. 8:31
[71]Lk. 22:69.   [72]Apoc. 1:13; 14:14.   [73]Dan. 7:13; 10:5 ff.
and Lk. 9:22 with Matt. 16:21; Lk. 6:22 with Matt. 5:11; Lk. 12:8
with Matt. 10:32.   [75]cf. Mk. 3:28; Eph. 3:5.

6

in their turn had difficulty in understanding it and most often regarded it as Jesus' way of emphasizing the lowliness involved in his state as man. This approach, which has been frequently taken up by modern scholars, has a great deal of truth in it, and is backed by the authority of a large number of texts in the gospels where the term appears in passages which emphasize the lowly and painful position of the saviour. For instance, we may cite the following passages : 'the Son of Man has nowhere to lay his head'[76]; he 'has come eating and drinking'[77] like any other man; he has come 'not to be served, but to serve',[78] and above all the repeated predictions of the passion in which it is always the 'Son of Man' who must suffer, be condemned, and die.[79] This interpretation is nevertheless much too narrow for the even greater number of instances in which the title 'Son of Man' is closely connected with a glorious and even transcendent destiny; not only will he rise from the dead—as the prophecies of the passion just referred to say, (and see also Matt. 17:9 and Mk. 9:9); but he will also come again in triumph. His second coming—the Parousia—will be as sudden as a flash of lightning;[80] on that day when he will reveal himself,[81] his sign will appear in the sky;[82] he will come then with his angels on the clouds, in great power and glory—the glory of his Father—and will take his place on the throne of glory to reward every man according to the way he has lived.[83] At this solemn judgement, he will send his angels

[76]Matt. 8:20 and Lk. 9:58.   [77]Matt. 11:19 and Lk. 7:34.
[78]Matt. 20:28 and Mk. 10:45.
[79]Mk. 8:31 and Lk. 9:22; Matt. 17:12 and Mk. 9:12; Matt. 17:22; Mk. 9:31; and Lk. 9:44; Matt. 20:18; Mk. 10:33 and Lk. 18:31; see also Matt. 26:2, 24, 45 and parallels; Lk. 24:7.
[80]Matt. 24:27 and Lk. 17:24; see also Matt. 24:37 and Lk. 17:26; Matt. 24:44 and Lk. 12:40.
[81]Lk. 17:30.   [82]Matt. 24:30.
[83]Matt. 16:27 and 25:31; cf. Mk. 8:38 and Lk. 9:26.

to purify his Kingdom,[84] to arraign all men before him;[85] his judgement will be that of the shepherd who picks out the good and bad from the flock;[86] he will acknowledge those who acknowledged him and will deny those who denied him.[87] Hence if the title Son of Man is no more than an expression of Christ's lowly state, it is difficult to see why it should be so prominent in these passages which so obviously endow it with a glorious eschatological importance. There is one statement Jesus made, however, which suggests that we look for some other explanation. This is the word he spoke before the Sanhedrin at the most solemn moment of his earthly career when the rulers of his people called upon him to give an explanation of what he was. He then not only admitted that he was 'the Christ, the Son of the Blessed'—that is, the Son of God, as Matthew explains—a claim which as we have already seen could possibly be understood of the human Messiah in Jewish tradition; but he added: 'Hereafter you will see the Son of Man seated at the right hand of the Power and coming on the clouds of heaven.'[88] His words greatly clarify the other texts we have mentioned and are an explicit manifestation of the deeper motive that influenced Jesus to call himself the Son of Man. There is no doubt that when he spoke in this way he was referring in the first place to Psalm 110, but more especially to Daniel 7 : 13. For in this text, for the first time in Jewish tradition, a Son of man appears in an eschatological context. In Daniel's vision, the 'Son of Man' comes on the clouds and moves towards the 'Ancient', who is God, and receives from him dominion, glory and kingship over all nations for ever. According to the angel's explanation of this

---

[84]Matt. 13:41.   [85]Lk. 21:36; Matt. 25:32.
[86]Matt. 25:32-46.   [87]Lk. 12:8 ff; Matt. 10:32 ff.
[88]Matt. 26:64; and see Mk. 14:62; Lk. 22:69.

vision, the 'Son of Man' must be seen in connexion with the
people 'of the saints of the Most High', in other words the
eschatological Israel.[89] This symbol, if we may draw on
modern research into corporate personality, must describe
both the people and its head; the Son of Man is more than
merely the personification of a group, he is in addition, for
Daniel, a particular person who at once sums up and represents his people, even as the fallen empires with their animal
symbols are visualized in the person of their rulers. In other
words we can see the emergence with Daniel of a concept of
the eschatological ruler of the chosen people radically different from that of the traditional Messiah, an earthly king,
scion of David's lineage who destroyed his enemies in war.
The new ruler is a transcendent personality of heavenly
origin, who has been given power to govern by the immediate
and supreme intervention of God. It will not be necessary for
us to explain at this point the events in the history of Israel
which account for such a fundamental change in its messianic hope, nor need we probe outside influences, from
Persia for example, which would have fostered it. The contemporary state of affairs and trends of thought might well
have been used by God in his ordinary scheme of revelation
to advance the ideas of his people and to prepare for the
complete realization of his design in Christ. What is important is for us to note this new direction in biblical tradition—
one which Jesus seems to have adopted.

This passage in Daniel is the only one where this idea
appears. Isaiah had described the glorious qualities of the
future King : 'Wonderful Counsellor, Mighty God, Everlasting Father';[90] and Psalm 110 had pictured him seated
at the right hand of God. But his human origin had never
been in doubt,[91] and he had never been called the 'Son of

[89]Daniel 7:18 and 27.
[90]Is. 9:5 ff; see also Mic. 5:1.   [91]Is. 7:14.

Man'. But the title, and the heavenly origin mentioned by
Daniel, does appear again in later Jewish tradition, particularly in the parables of Henoch where even more stress is laid
on his transcendent nature and pre-existence; for example
'the Son of Man was named in the presence of the Lord of
spirits ... before the sun and the signs were created, before
the stars of heaven were made, his name was named before
the Lord of spirits'.[92] The Semitic origin of the text implies
that 'to be named' is 'to exist.' He is identified with the
Chosen One 'hidden before the Lord before the creation of
the world and for eternity '(Henoch 48:6). Although his
nature derives from heaven, it seems that he must also have
an earthly existence in order to carry out a mission of salvation, for 'this is the Son of Man who has righteousness and
with whom righteousness dwells, and who reveals all the
treasures of that which is hidden, because the Lord of spirits
has chosen him and his choice has won through by the right
which he has from the Lord of spirits for evermore' (Henoch,
46:3).

He will be a staff for the righteous on which they will
support themselves and not fall, and he will be the light
of the gentiles and the hope of those who are troubled of
heart. All who dwell on earth will fall down and bow the
knee before him and will bless and praise and celebrate
with song the Lord of spirits. . . . And the wisdom of the
Lord of spirits has revealed him to the holy and righteous
. . . . for they are saved in his name and he is the avenger
of their life (Henoch, 48:4-5, 7).

Ultimately he will be the judge :

[92]*Parables of Henoch,* 48:2 ff., *Eng. ed.* R. H. Charles, op. cit.,
vol. II, p. 185, 216 etc.

And there shall stand up in that day all the kings and the mighty and the exalted and those who hold the earth, and they shall recognize and see how he sits on the throne of his glory, and righteousness is judged before him. . . . And he will deliver them to the angels for punishment, to execute vengeance on them because they have oppressed his children and his elect. . . . But the righteous and the elect shall be saved on that day and they shall never henceforth see the faces of the sinners and unrighteous. And the Lord of spirits will abide over them, and with that Son of Man shall they eat and lie down and rise up for ever. . . . They (the just) will all become angels in heaven. (Henoch, 62:3,11, 13, 14; 51:4).

Passages like these cast an astonishing light upon many of Jesus' statements, and some scholars have found the resemblances so striking as to force upon them the conclusion that, if the parables of Henoch did not have a Christian origin, they at least underwent a considerable revision at the hands of Christians. The 'interpolations' in this hypothesis must have been done by someone of great ability and great tact, because he makes none of those too apparent allusions which usually betray additions to the text. Hence, on the whole, critics strongly maintain the Jewish origin of this part of the book of Henoch. The ideas it expresses can well be understood as the effluence of a new current of thought inspired by Daniel; other tributaries of this stream could be quoted, such as 4 Esdras, chapter 13; not to mention others which may now be lost. For in the eyes of orthodox Judaism represented by the Pharisees, true to the traditional messianism of the Davidic king,[93] this was a heretical form of eschatology;

[93]See 'Psalms of Solomon' 17, in *Epigrapha and Pseudoepigrapha of the Old Testament*, R. H. Charles, op. cit., vol. II.

and with the triumph of Rabbinism their views prevailed and all others fell into obscurity.

When scholars cast doubt on this view of the Son of Man, what really lies behind their hesitation is the fear that to admit such a view prior to the time of Jesus would be to detract from his originality. But this fear is ill-founded. The originality of Jesus did not consist in expounding completely new ideas, unconnected with the previous tradition of his people—in that case they never could have been accepted nor even understood. His originality lay in combining and harmonizing widely differing ideas which flowed in parallel streams in Jewish tradition; in perfecting and fulfilling those concepts which were for the most part no better than rough and inconsistent sketches; and above all in giving them concrete expression in his own Person, a goal to which he was led by the profound awareness he possessed of his nature and mission. In every page of the gospel we feel that he had meditated deeply on the Old Testament prophecies and had made them his own; we may be equally sure that he was alive to the hopes current in contemporary Judaism, and the recent discoveries at Qumrân will probably make it clear that he knew the doctrines of the Essenes. These hopes and doctrines were not the determining cause of his consciousness of what he was; this consciousness sprang from the depths of his own transcendent personality and from his relationship with his Father; but he used them to explain himself to his contemporaries; from them he drew that form of speech which alone could reach their minds, and bring the message of revelation to its term. God spoke 'at different times in various ways',[94] giving increasing light to his people in their progress on the way of salvation; these rays of light are partial glimpses of a truth which is continually develop-

[94]Hebrews 1:1.

ing, continually trying to find itself, and they are apparently irreconcilable in their variety; but if we take seriously the economy of the Word, it is a source of wonder to see these partial truths come together and find perfect expression in one who harmonizes and fulfils them all in his own person. This is what came to pass in Jesus.

Some Jews were expecting a Messiah of David's house, and so Jesus accepted the title 'Son of David', admitted quite explicitly that he was the Christ, while avoiding the political overtones implied in the word.[95] Isaiah had spoken of a Servant whose sufferings and death would expiate the sins of men; there can be no doubt that Jesus consciously took upon himself this role.[96] Again, other Jews, for example Daniel and the movement (cf. the *Parables of Henoch*) he initiated, focused their hope on a transcendental Son of Man of heavenly origin, commissioned to bring justice and salvation. Jesus used this title and in doing so deliberately identified himself with that eschatological figure.

He chose to single out this title, and his preference transmuted all the earlier notions about the Messiah. He was indeed 'son of David', but in the sense of Psalm 110, as the one who was raised to the right hand of God and thus became David's Lord.[97] He was truly Servant, endowed with the fullness of God's favour;[98] but he was such in his condition of Son, as the Voice from heaven proclaimed at his baptism[99] and transfiguration.[100] In calling himself 'Son of Man', Jesus not only attributed to himself the role of eschatological Judge[101] (which itself far exceeded the prerogative of the

[95]Mk. 10:47 and parallels; cf. Matt. 9:27; 12:23; 15:22; 21:9, 15.
[96]Mk. 10:45; 14:24 and parallels. Lk. 22:37; see Matt. 3:17; 8:17; 12:8-21.
[97]Matt. 22:41-46; 26:64 and parallels.   [98]Is. 42:1.
[99]Matt. 3:17 and parallels.   [100]Matt. 17:5 and parallels.
[101]Mk. 8:38 and parallels; Matt. 10:32 ff. and Lk. 12:8 ff; Matt. 13:41; 25:31-46; Lk. 21:36.

traditional Messiah); but he also announced that he was even now this Person of heavenly origin endowed with divine powers, saying, for example, that : 'the Son of Man has authority on earth to forgive sins',[102] or that he is 'lord of the Sabbath'.[103] He allowed the awareness of his own pre-existence to become revealed eventually in the mysterious 'I have come' utterances which in the synoptic gospels have even more significance for their being so Joannine in tone. We read, for example, 'I have come not to abolish but to fulfil';[104] 'I have not come to bring peace but a sword';[105] 'the Son of Man came not to be served but to serve';[106] 'the Son of Man came to seek out and save the lost'.[107] The words could mean simply 'to come in public', 'to manifest oneself'; but they suggest much more when they are compared with similar but clearer sayings in John : 'I have come into the world'; 'I have come that the flock may have life'.[108]

The most diverse texts of the gospel come together in this way to form an impression which is almost unavoidable. They bear witness to the fact that Jesus called himself and believed himself to be more than the Messiah-Son of David, more than the Suffering Servant of Jahweh, to be in fact the pre-existent and eschatological Son of Man. His words are illuminated by his deep awareness of his character as Son, in intimate union with the Father, and they in turn cast light on this awareness; and in this light they point to the conclusion that he thought of himself as the heavenly, divine person proclaimed by the Scriptures, and that this is what he taught.

[102]Mk. 2:10 and parallels.   [103]Mark 2:28 and parallels.
[104]Matt. 5:17.   [105]Matt. 10:34; cf. Lk. 12:49-51.
[106]Mk. 10:45 and Matt. 20:28.
[107]Lk. 19:10. See also Matt. 8:29; 9:13 and parallels; 10:35; and Lk. 4:43, where Mark's 'I have come forth' (1:38) is interpreted as 'I have been sent'.   [108]John 12:46; 18:37; 10:10.

The Mystery of Jesus

Could Jesus have expressed himself more clearly? For example could he have defined his being in the ontological terms of 'nature' and 'person'. as the theologians of the Church were later to do? Certainly not. These terms would be necessary later, to express his message in the forms of Greek thought. But they would have met with no response in the field where he was 'sowing the Word'.[109] He left the task of cultivating the crop to the future, while he sowed the seed which the land was able to receive.[110] Yet even then, though his teaching was couched in imagery taken from his people's own way of life, it was difficult enough to grasp. He proclaimed a 'mystery', 'a secret' penetrable only in virtue of a revelation of the Father.[111] Many men would find it 'a stumbling block'[112] and would be partly excused[113] because of the human appearances which cloaked its mysterious reality.

We have seen that expectation of a Son of Man had already won admittance in some devout Jewish circles, but we must not be led to think that it was widely held outside their private assemblies. The crowd were evidently not aware of it, otherwise they would not have asked 'and who is this Son of Man?'[114] The better informed Jewish leaders, who guessed well enough what was at stake, pressed Jesus into making the claim to be the heavenly person, though they themselves refused to share this expectation. When Jesus formally made his claim before them, the members of the Sanhedrin were shocked at the blasphemy, and from their point of view they were perfectly justified. To claim to be Messiah, in their traditional and orthodox sense, would not

[109]Matt. 13:17.   [110]Mk. 4:26-29; see also 4:30-32.
[111]Mk. 4:11 and parallels; Matt. 11:27 ff. and Lk. 10:22 ff; Matt. 16:17.
[112]Cf. Matt. 11:6 and Lk. 7:23.   [113]Matt. 12:32 and Lk. 12:10.
[114]John 12:34; cf. Matt. 16:13-14 and parallels.

have involved blasphemy; but it was clear that Jesus was claiming much more—he was putting himself on the same level as God. In comparing himself to Daniel's Son of Man, he gave the title Son of God a new, transcendental, non-metaphorical meaning which their strict monotheism could not tolerate.[115] For that reason they sentenced him to death.

The disciples themselves, even during his life, had the feeling that their Master was more than the Messiah. There was something divine in the authority of his words, the power of his actions, and the dazzling quality of his personality. They clearly knew better than the crowd the real meaning of 'Son of Man'. Nevertheless Jesus' humanity remained a very difficult mask to pierce; the mystery surrounding him could not be completely dispersed while they saw him living among them, as one of themselves. They needed the passion to make them understand that he was the true suffering Servant who atoned for the sin of the world. They also needed the resurrection and the coming of the Holy Spirit to give conviction to their belief that he truly belonged to the world of God. After they had been given evidence that he had risen godward through his victorious exaltation, it slowly dawned on them, under the Holy Spirit's guidance, that he had always belonged there, and that from thence he had come to them, only to return once more. The thinkers 'among them, like Paul and John, began then to discover new perspectives in the Scriptures which cast light on his incarnation. This was a whole field for their faith to conquer, extending the revelation of Jesus and making explicit what it had not been possible for him to say outright.[116] It was not, however, the 'fabrication of a myth', alien to his thought, as too many critics believe, but rather the penetration of mysteries which he had enunciated during his life-time but which were in-

[115]See Lk. 22:70; John 19:7; Matt. 27:40, 43.
[116]Cf. John 14:25 ff. and 16:12 ff.

comprehensible at the time—the growth of the seed he had
sown. It was, under the guidance of the Spirit, the flowering
of revelation which had begun in the Old Testament, had
reached full-growth in Jesus, and was now ready to bear
fruit in the full realization of the divine plan. This final stage
of the development has the force of a revelation which is
normative for our faith. This evolution is reflected in the
New Testament writings, and the essays which follow will
trace its progress. It has been enough to show here that even
as early as the synoptic gospels—in that very ancient echo
of the first kerygma—we can find all the basic elements of
the earliest Christian faith. This teaching is still veiled, for
Jesus could not give the full revelation of his being before the
passion and resurrection. It is also incomplete, because
popular preaching, which the synoptists reproduce, was less
concerned with their master's deep and difficult sayings; St
John was more concerned with them. But it is still clear
enough to assure us that Jesus presented himself as the Messiah, the Saviour, the pre-existent and eschatological Son of
Man, and above all as the Son of God, in the proper meaning of the word.

The Divinity of Christ in Saint Paul

M. E. Boismard O.P.

IV

The Divinity of Christ in Saint Paul

M. E. Boismard O.P.

PAUL RARELY REFERS to Christ as God, but reserves this name for the Father; the Father was 'God' *par excellence,* he who had been worshipped by the Jews for centuries without rival of any kind.[1] Their fierce monotheism had its roots in the first Commandment of Exodus 20 : 2-4, and found its most perfect formulation in the words of Deuteronomy :

Hear Israel, Jahweh our God
Is the only God.

We discover an exact echo of this profession of belief in a single God coming from Paul's pen : 'we know that an idol has no real existence and that there is no God but one . . . for us there is one God, the Father . . . from whom all things come and for whom we all exist'.[2]

[1]Two texts are exceptions to this. The doxology of Romans 9:5 is one, where the word 'God' ought grammatically to refer to Christ. This interpretation has, however, been a perpetual bone of contention, and many scholars, some of them Catholics, would rather have it refer to the Father. In face of such ambiguity, it would be imprudent to cite this text as apodictic proof of Paul's belief in the divinity of Christ. The second passage is in the Letter to Titus: 'We are awaiting our blessed (?) hope, the appearing of the glory of our great God and Saviour, Jesus Christ who gave himself to redeem us,' etc. (2:13). This text *can* be translated in what is the RSV alternative, 'the showing forth of the great God, and the Saviour, Jesus Christ. . . .' It must also be borne in mind that the immediately Pauline authorship of the Pastoral Letters is not undisputed.

[2]1 Cor. 8:4-6. Cf. Eph. 4:6.

The one God has, however, a Son, Jesus the Christ, a fact which Paul frequently asserts : 'God has sent his Son . . . he did not spare his own Son, but gave him up for us all' (Rom. 8 : 3-32). God, he writes, has called us 'into the fellowship of his Son, Jesus Christ our Lord' (1 Cor. 1 : 9); he has made us pass over 'from the dominion of darkness to the kingdom of his beloved Son' (Col. 1 : 13). Christ is thus 'Son of God' (Rom. 1 : 4), 'the Son of God' (2 Cor. 1 : 19).[3] He is pre-eminently 'the Son'.

Yet how are we to understand this special relationship between Christ and the one God of Judaism? Can we assume that in Paul's mind Jesus was God himself, possessing an equal godhead with his Father? Paul's belief in the divinity of Christ can hardly be called in question, but some scholars have held the view that his conception of Christ was derived from the many 'heroes' of the pagan world; in other words that Christ was born a man, but was divinized after his death. Hence the myth of the Christ-God would have its origin in the belief in the Risen Christ, and it was Paul who would have been chiefly responsible for this apotheosis.

In the following pages we shall try to find out exactly, firstly, the place which the fact of Christ's resurrection and exaltation occupied in Saint Paul's christology, and secondly, the sense in which he understood the pre-existence of Christ, Son of God.

In both sections it will be important to stress the connexions between Paul's thought and the primitive apostolic preaching, which is in turn based on the teaching of Christ. We shall then be able to see that Paul found the essence of his faith in Jesus the Son of God in primitive Christian tradition.

---

[3]Cf. also Gal. 2:20; Eph. 4:13.

A. THE RESURRECTION AND EXALTATION OF CHRIST

The Resurrection of Christ

The whole of primitive Christian thought, including Paul's, was dominated and directed by the fact of the resurrection. The Apostle himself, it is true, did not see the Risen Christ in the appearances which took place from time to time between the resurrection and the ascension, but there are several passages in his letters in which he claims the privilege of having seen the Risen Christ (1 Cor. 9 : 1) and considers that this vision of his is of the same kind as those which came immediately after the resurrection (1 Cor. 15 :8). This crucial event, which changed the course of his life, happened when one day he was on the road to Damascus, bent on harassing the followers of Christ there. Hurled to the ground by a mysterious power, while a blinding light shone around him, he heard a voice saying : 'I am Jesus, whom you are persecuting'.[4] Paul had frequently heard the witness of those he hated and persecuted : 'This Jesus whom you sent to his death, has been raised up again by God; we are witnesses of it'; but he had always considered them liars. On that day the truth struck him blind. Jesus was actually there, alive, before his eyes, surrounded by an aura of light and of glory. Paul then understood, in a blinding flash of inspiration that would leave its mark on him for life, that Jesus was indeed the Messiah, the triumphant Head of the Kingdom of God, as his followers had proclaimed. More than that, he saw the splendour of the light around him, light not unlike the mysterious glory which had always been characteristic of the presence of God. He was hurled to the ground by the power which irradiated from that glory, as it had done in the appearances of God in the Old Testament—not only was Jesus of Naza-

---

[4]Acts 9:3-5; 22:6-8; 26:13-15. Cf. 1 Cor. 9:1; 15:8.

7

reth risen from the dead, but he now belonged to the supernatural world, the dwelling place of God.

The Exaltation of the Son

The realization of this truth was to be the directing and
fructifying principle in the evolution of the apostle's
thought. Basically, the resurrection, as far as the apostles
were concerned, had constituted the coming of God's Kingdom and the enthronement of the Messiah as its head. In
Israel and throughout the ancient East, we must remember,
a king's enthronement thereby placed him in a position of
particular intimacy with God : he became the Son of God;
God became his father.[5] This idea finds magnificent expression in Psalm 2, where on the day of his coronation the
Messiah-King hears God telling him :

> You are my Son;
> I have begotten you today.

These words were quite commonly applied to the resurrection of Christ, which had constituted him King and enthroned him over the new Israel. Paul does so quite explicitly
in his first sermon before the Jewish leaders in Antioch at
the outset of his first missionary journey : 'And we bring
you the good news that what God promised to the fathers,
this he had fulfilled to us their children by raising Jesus; as
also it is written in the second psalm, "You are my Son; I
have begotten you today" ' (Acts 13 :32-33).
In the Old Testament the meaning of this expression always remained merely metaphorical. But Jesus, as we have
noted, had already applied the title 'Son of God' to himself in
a quite exceptional way. Now, the apostles had seen Christ

---

[5]Cf. 1 Sam. 7:14; Ps. 89:27-28.

resplendent with light and glory, transported by his resurrection to the sphere of the divine, 'seated at the right hand of God', according to the expression of Psalm 110 quoted by our Lord : and this experience made Paul, in particular, realize that the title 'Son of God' must be applied to the risen Christ enthroned as king in a real, and not a metaphorical, sense. This becomes quite clear as we read the texts in which Paul speaks of Christ exalted in glory.

In the prologue to the letter to the Romans, where the dominant ideas and language recall the sermon of Acts quoted above, Paul once again stresses the connexion between the resurrection and the divine Sonship of Christ : 'Paul a servant of Jesus Christ, called to be an apostle, set apart for the gospel of God ... the gospel concerning his Son who was descended from David according to the flesh and constituted Son of God in power according to the Spirit of holiness, by his resurrection from the dead, Jesus Christ, our Lord '(1 : 1-4). Paul here contrasts the two successive 'states' in Christ's existence. He was born of David's race in becoming man; he was made Son of God by his resurrection.[6] In Ephesians, the apostle dwells on the power of God which brought about Christ's resurrection and exaltation. He wrote the following verses which give a tremendous impression of power :

May the God of our Lord Jesus Christ give you a spirit of

[6]In order to avoid making Paul say that Jesus was only designated Son of God at his resurrection, as though he were not that beforehand, most modern scholars would add the phrase 'in power' to the title 'Son of God'. The sense would then be that Christ was designated 'Son of God in power' at his resurrection, that is, he was once again restored to the power that was his in virtue of his being Son of God—a power of which he divested or 'emptied' himself when he was crucified. But the other texts quoted here make it clear that Paul means: 'He was made Son of God', without restriction. How this formula is to be explained, we shall see later.

wisdom and of revelation in the knowledge of him, having
the eyes of your hearts enlightened, that you may know . . .
what is the immeasurable greatness of his power in us who
believe, according to the working of his great might which
he accomplished in Christ when he raised him from the
dead and made him sit at his right hand in the heavenly
places, far above all rule and authority and power and
dominion, and above every name that is named not only
in this age but also in that which is to come (Eph. 1. 18-
21).

As the result of his resurrection, Christ was, therefore,
exalted above every 'name', that is, above every existing
thing[7]—so was he placed in the hierarchy of heavenly
beings. Such an exaltation 'above every name' must have
some bearing on the name 'Son of God' mentioned in the
letter to the Romans; and indeed the connexion was shown
in its clarity by the author of the letter to the Hebrews who
was an accurate transmitter of Paul's thought:

He reflects the glory of God and bears the very stamp of
his nature, upholding the universe by his word of power.
When he had made purification for sins, he sat down at
the right hand of the Majesty on high, having become as
much superior to angels as the name he has obtained is
more excellent than theirs. For to what angel did God ever
say, 'You are my Son. Today I have begotten you' (Heb.
1 : 3-5).

The title Son of God, which Christ could use of himself
was therefore no mere title of honour, but the name which

---

[7] A name, for Semitic peoples, is more than the label it is with
Europeans. It is the expression of a person's total nature and personality, it is, one might say, the substitute for the person.

proclaims his position in the hierarchy of living beings, a position over all heavenly beings, 'not only in this world, but also in the world to come'.

The identical thought also found expression in the hymn to Christ in the letter to the Philippians, which describes the whole career of Christ in a thrilling summary :

Though he (Christ) was in the form of God, he did not count equality with God a prize to be grasped, but emptied himself, taking the form of a servant being born in the likeness of men. And being found in human form he humbled himself and became obedient unto death, even death on a cross. Therefore God has highly exalted him and bestowed on him the name which is above every name, that at the name of Jesus every knee should bow, in heaven and on earth and under the earth, and every tongue confess that Jesus Christ is *Lord*, in the glory of God the Father (Phil. 2 :6-11).

Reference will be made later to the beginning of this hymn but it is enough for us to comment here on its internal structure. Paul first describes Christ's successive 'emptyings' of himself—he became like men, and much more than that, he died on a cross! The apostle then contrasts with this emptying, the exaltation Christ won by his resurrection and the name he received from God as his right. The leading themes of the letters to the Romans and the Philippians are found here, but they are nowhere else expressed so strongly —Christ has not had *any* name bestowed on him, but 'the name which is above every name'. Verse 11 leads most people to think that the name would be that of *Kyrios*, Lord; yet M. Cerfaux is undoubtedly correct when he considers that, coming from the pen of a Hebrew, 'the name which is above every name' can only mean the transcendent name of the

God of the Old Testament, Jahweh, a name which the Jews dared not utter.[8] We can, consequently, appreciate that every being, the whole of the created universe, must bend the knee as a symbol of adoration before this name. Yet if Christ is called Son of God because he has been given the name of Jahweh, the Old Testament's special name for God, it surely follows that he can claim the privilege of being regarded as the equal of the one God.

Earlier essays in this book have shown that 'to be seated at the right hand of God' implied a certain equality with God as far as the Jews were concerned. And it was because Christ claimed that equal standing with God that he was sentenced to death as a blasphemer and, later, Stephen was stoned by the Jews for the same reason. We only have to recall the embarrassment of the Pharisees when Christ asked them: 'How can the scribes say that the Christ is the Son of David (i.e. no more than a man)? David himself, inspired by the Holy Spirit declared, "Jahweh said to my Lord sit at my right hand till I put your enemies under your feet"' (Mark 12 :35-36). The embarrassment of the scribes quite clearly showed that this prophetic text took it for granted that the Messiah was God and not just man, that he was *Kyrios,* the Lord. Saint Paul, then, is only using Christ's own words, understanding them as Christ himself had understood them, when he places Christ above all beings at the right hand of God, and bestows upon him the name Jahweh, which is above every name, a name proper to the God of the Old Testament, a name the Septuagint translates as *Kyrios,* Lord.

At the right hand of God

Paul was no revolutionary in stating this belief. He was no

_____

[8] In *Le Christ dans le theologie de S. Paul,* (Paris, 1951), pp. 296 and 352. The literary connexion between this hymn to Christ and many chapters of the Deutero-Isaiah is especially intriguing.

more than repeating a solemn declaration of Christ himself, as the first Christian communities had done before him. Jesus, in the presence of the High Priest, on the morning of his death, was solemnly asked, 'Are you the Christ, the Son of the Blessed?' He replied, 'I am, and you will see the Son of Man *sitting at the right hand of Power*' (Mk. 14:62). In this reply he applies the messianic prophecy of Psalm 110 to himself: 'Jahweh said to my Lord, *Sit at my right hand* till I put your enemies under your feet.' From the day of Pentecost the apostles had realized that Christ's exaltation 'to the right hand of God' had become a fact on Easter day. We see this in Peter's use of the same text of Psalm 110 (Acts 2:32-36). When Paul wrote to the Romans (8:34): 'Christ Jesus, who died, yes, who was raised from the dead, *who is at the right hand of God,* who intercedes for us', he seems to be doing no more than repeating a formula used in primitive apostolic preaching. He uses these same words of Psalm 110 to describe the exaltation of Christ in the passage from his letter to Ephesus (1:20) quoted already: 'He raised him (Christ) from the dead, and made him *sit at his right hand* in the heavenly places.' He also wrote this to Colossae (3:1): 'If then you have been raised with Christ, seek the things that are above, where Christ is, *seated at the right hand of God.*' The author of the letter to Hebrews says the same thing in a passage we have also already quoted (1:3): 'When he had made purification for sins, he *sat down at the right hand* of *the Majesty* on high.' Hence the exaltation of which Paul speaks is the same as that which Christ had announced, the same as that which the psalmist had prophesied.

Christ and the Prophecies of the Old Testament

If then, Christ has been given the 'Name which is above every name', the name of the only God, then Old Testament texts concerning Jahweh, the Lord, can also be applied to him. Paul himself never hesitated to do so, sometimes explicitly quoting these texts, sometimes clearly alluding to them.

In the hymn in the letter to the Philippians, on which we have already remarked, Paul ends with these words : 'at the name of Jesus *every knee should bow* in heaven and on earth, and *every tongue confess* that Jesus Christ is Lord'. The words in italics are quite clearly borrowed from the prophecies of Isaiah through whose mouth God proclaims :

> To me every knee shall bow,
> Every tongue shall swear (Is. 45:23).

The prophet's words occur in a context which deals exclusively with the praise of God, the one God, the Saviour. Jahweh is creator of heaven and earth, he alone formed them (Is. 45 : 18-19). He is the one God, Jahweh, and idols are nothing in his sight (vv. 20-22); he alone can save his enslaved people (vv. 23-25); pagan idols will all fall into decay (46 : 1-4); and Jahweh will remain the only God, without peer, without rival (vv. 5 : 10).[9] It is therefore because he is the one God, the only God, **that** 'every knee shall bow before him and every tongue confess that he is God'. If then Paul—the Rabbi brought up in the school of Gamaliel, for whom the Word of God was food and drink—if Paul applies these words of adoration of Jahweh the only God to Christ, he must have been quite certain that Jesus Christ was God, equal to Jahweh in virtue of the 'Name above every name' bestowed upon him. To the name of Jesus every knee must bend, and every tongue must confess that Jesus Christ is 'Lord' : this is the title by which the Greek Septuagint used by Paul translates the ineffable name Jahweh.

[9]Cf. 45:5: 'I am Jahweh, God, and there is no other; beside me there is *no* God.

There is a similar example in the letter to the Romans, in a context which forcibly recalls the letter to the Philippians. Paul begins by stating : 'If you confess (acknowledge) with your lips that Jesus is Lord and believe in your heart that God raised him from the dead, you will be saved' (10 : 9). The first part of this extract is reminiscent of the phrase in Philippians: 'that every tongue should confess that Jesus is Lord'; it is moreover the expression of one of the oldest confessions of the Christian faith. But in Romans Paul directs our attention to the idea of salvation : he who professes that Jesus is Lord will be saved. To express this, he uses a text from the Old Testament : 'For all men (Jew and Gentile) there is one Lord, who bestows his riches on all who call him : *for all those who call on the name of the Lord shall be saved*' (10 : 12-13); and the prophet Joel had written, speaking of messianic times and the outpouring of the Spirit : 'And it shall come to pass that *all who call upon the name of the Lord (Jahweh) will be saved*' (Joel 3 : 5). Paul, therefore, takes up this prophecy word by word : but whereas, for the prophet, the name of the Lord was the name of Jahweh the one God of the Old Testament, Paul applies the text to Christ, in virtue of the principle that 'the Name above every name', the name of Jahweh, had been bestowed upon him.

Here again it would be quite wrong to suppose that Paul has introduced any innovation. The application of the Old Testament phrase 'calling upon the name of the Lord (Jahweh)' to Christ has its origin in the beginnings of Christianity itself. Paul wrote in his first letter to the Corinthians : 'Paul, called by the will of God to be an apostle . . . to the church of God which is at Corinth . . . together with those who in every place *call on the name of the Lord Jesus Christ,* both their Lord and ours' (1 : 1-2). This formulary seems to indicate quite clearly a Christian custom of characterizing themselves as 'the ones who call upon the name of Jesus'.

Confirmation of this is found in two passages of Acts where we discover that even before Paul's conversion, the Christians of the different communities in Palestine designated themselves as, 'those who call upon the Name (of the Lord Jesus)'. On this point Fr. Allo writes: 'It is most important to notice here that it was the invocation of the name of Jesus Christ which was the source of Christian unity, in the same way that the invocation of Jahweh's name was the source of Jewish unity. They clearly adored Jesus as God'.[10]

It is possible to discover in Acts the origin of the application to Christ of the text of Joel: 'Whoever calls upon the Name of the Lord will be saved'. The lame beggar at the Temple gate was healed by Peter with these words: 'In the name of Jesus Christ, walk!'; and the man was made healthy again only by the invoking of Jesus' name, as Peter goes on to explain to the Jews who had crowded round to see the wonder done:

> Men of Israel, why do you wonder at this, or why do you stare at us, as though by our own power or piety we had made him walk? The God of Abraham and of Isaac and of Jacob, the God of our fathers glorified his servant Jesus ... whom God raised from the dead. To this we are witnesses. And his name, our faith in his name, has made this man strong ... (Acts 3 : 12-16).

A little later on, Peter alludes again to the healing of this lame man, when he protests to the Sanhedrin:

> That it is by the name of Jesus Christ of Nazareth, whom you crucified, whom God raised from the dead, that this man is standing before you well. . . . And there is salvation

[10]In his commentary on 1 Corinthians in *Etudes Bibliques*.

in no one else, for there is no other name under heaven given to men by which we must be saved (Acts 4 : 10-13).

Thus the miracle performed 'in the Name of Jesus' clearly substantiated the fact that the Name of the Jesus, who, in rising from the dead, was exalted by God, brought about the salvation of men. Jesus then, in his glorified person, clearly fulfilled what the prophets of old had said of Jahweh : 'Whoever calls upon the name of the Lord will be saved' (Joel 3 : 5). This association of ideas was all the more striking in that the lame man was healed only a few days after Pentecost, the day on which took place the outpouring of the Spirit which Joel (Joel 3 : 1-5) gave as the sign of the beginning of the messianic era, the era of salvation through the invocation of the name of Jahweh (Acts 2 : 17 ff).

In his second letter to the Christians at Corinth, Paul contrasts the two covenants, the Old Testament established by God on Sinai in the person of Moses and the New Testament established in the person of Christ. The pivot of the apostle's whole argument is the passage in Exodus which describes the appearance of God on Sinai when he revealed himself to Moses and openly showed him his glory (Ex. 34). When he came down from the holy mountain, Moses had to veil his face, which was ablaze with the glory of God, to avoid terrifying the Israelites. Whenever Moses went into the Tent of Meeting to speak with God, he removed the veil : 'But whenever Moses entered the presence of the Lord (Jahweh) to speak with him, he took the veil off, until he came out' (34 : 34). Paul takes up this text and applies it to the Jews of his own time who, having been converted to Christ come to understand the Scriptures. The Scriptures are thus 'unveiled' for them : 'Yes, to this day, whenever Moses is read a veil lies over their minds, but when a man

turns to the Lord, the veil is removed' (2 Cor. 3 : 16). And so
the Christian is rather like Moses; his uncovered face reflects
'the glory of the Lord'. Christ has taken the place of God who
revealed himself on Sinai, because God has glorified him,
bestowing on him the glory which in the Old Testament was
characteristic of the divine, and which was indeed the visible
showing forth of his own invisible and infinite nature.

The prophets in their writings had often proclaimed the
coming of Jahweh, at the end of time, to pass judgement
either on his own faithless people or on the nations who
persecuted them. Later the idea took on a more general
meaning, and it was thought that God would come to judge
all the wicked, whether they belonged to the Chosen People
or not. The prophets had coined a technical term to describe
the day of God's coming as judge. They called it the 'Day of
Anger' or better 'The Day of Jahweh' (the Septuagint calls
it 'The Day of the Lord'). Paul takes up the phrase in his
letter to the Romans, where it is God (i.e. the Father) who
will come in judgement 'on the day of wrath, when God's
righteous judgement will be revealed' (Rom. 2 : 5).

However it is more frequently Christ who assumes the
office of Judge in place of the God of the Old Testament.
Paul, without making any distinction between them, says
that we must all appear before the tribunal of God (Rom.
14 : 10), or the tribunal of Christ (2 Cor. 5 : 10); he speaks of
the day on which God (2 Thess. 1 : 6) or, equally, Christ
(Col. 3 : 24) will inflict punishment. The Day of Jahweh then
becomes in Paul's writings the Day of the Lord, in other
words, the Day of Christ.[11] The Apostle describes this 'Day
of the Lord' in his second letter to the Thessalonians, a description which is woven out of Old Testament allusions and
in which 'the Lord Jesus Christ' exactly replaces the Old

[11]Cf. 1 Cor. 1:7-8; 4:5; 5:5; 2 Cor. 1:14; Phil. 1:6, 10; 2:16;
1 Thess. 3:13; 4:15-16; 5:2, 23.

Testament 'Jahweh'. Note, moreover, that Paul begins with the idea of God (the Father) coming to pass judgement :

> Therefore we ourselves boast of you in the churches of God for your steadfastness and faith in all your persecutions and in the afflictions which you are enduring. This is evidence of the righteous *judgement of God,* that you may be made worthy of the kingdom of God, for which you are suffering—since indeed *God deems it just* to repay with affliction those who afflict you, and to grant rest with us to you who are afflicted (2 Thess. 1 :4-7).

But then he goes on to specify that in fact it is Christ who will exercise judgement on the 'Day of the Lord' :

> When the *Lord* Jesus is revealed from heaven with his mighty angels *in flaming fire, inflicting vengeance* upon those who do not know God and upon those who do not obey the gospel of our Lord Jesus. They shall suffer the punishment of eternal destruction and *exclusion from the face of the Lord and from the glory of his might, when he comes* on that day to be glorified in his saints, and to be marvelled at in all who have believed, because our testimony to you was believed (2 Thess. 1 :7-10).

This extract recalls the words of the prophet Isaiah, when he announced the Judgement of Jahweh :

> 'For behold the Lord (Jahweh) will come like a fire ... *to inflict vengeance* in his anger, to accomplish his threats *in flaming fire*' (Is. 66 :15); and again : 'Hide yourselves in the earth, *far from the face of the Lord, far from the*

glory of his power, when he comes to strike the earth . . .'
(Is. 2 : 10).

Paul ends by stating that this judgement will be 'so that
the name of our Lord Jesus may be glorified' (2 Thess. 2 : 12),
which are the exact words used by Isaiah : 'So that the Name
of Jahweh (the Lord) be glorified' (Is. 66 : 5). Here again
Paul is not innovating : Christ himself had proclaimed his
own eventual return in the glory of his Father to act as
judge over all men. The Old Testament awaited the
Parousia of Jahweh at the end of time; the one who comes,
as he himself had proclaimed, is Christ, taking the place of
Jahweh.

Lord and King

In all the texts we have examined, Christ is called 'the
Lord' by Paul yet, long before his letters had been written,
the earliest communities of Christians had summed up their
faith in the expression 'Jesus is Lord'. It is indeed possible to
find echoes of this primitive profession of faith in Paul's own
writings.[12] Cerfaux has very penetratingly observed that :

In primitive Christianity, 'Jesus is Lord' is tantamount to
affirming that Christ is reigning. The function that this
earliest and basic affirmation of Christian belief held is
indicated in the Aramaic formula which preserves it, and
Paul will recall this ancient profession of faith in his letters
. . . where we can yet find, in spite of all the other overtones, the ancient affirmation of the royal dignity of
Christ.[13]

[12]Rom. 10:9, 1 Cor. 12:3; cf. Phil. 2:11.
[13]Cerfaux, *'Le Christ dans la théologie de saint Paul'*, op. cit.,
p. 75.

The clearest text is undoubtedly Rom. 14 :9 : 'For to this end Christ died and lived again, that he might be Lord both of the dead and the living'. His dominion is not confined to men living on earth; it extends farther to all heavenly beings. Christ must be the head, the leader, who gathers together all things without exception under his power, be they upon earth or in heaven (Eph. 1 : 10). Finally, Christ must rule over the whole assemblage of Powers, the mysterious beings who in the old economy ruled the world and governed it. Paul pictures them as conquered by Christ and acting now as a foil to his royal apotheosis : 'He disarmed the principalities and powers and made a public example of them, dragging them in his triumphal procession' (Col. 2 : 15). Clearly Christ must reign and bring about the destruction one after the other of all the Powers inimical to him. This idea rests on the Psalmist's testimony : 'God has put everything under his (the Messiah's) feet',[14] and more especially upon Psalm 110, which had proclaimed by prophecy Christ's exaltation and triumph over all enemies :

Jahweh says to my lord :
Sit at my right hand,
Till I make your enemies your footstool.
Jahweh sends out from Zion
Your mighty sceptre.
Rule in the midst of your foes.

Hence Paul could state, in his turn : 'He (Christ) must reign until he has put all his enemies under his feet. The last enemy to be destroyed is death' (1 Cor. 15 :25-26). The Jews awaited the coming of the Kingdom of Jahweh, and Christ it was who came to be King of the world.

[14]Ps. 8:7; cf. 1 Cor. 15:27; Eph. 1:22.

Conclusion

In our endeavour to show that Jesus Christ, in Paul's eyes, was the equal of Jahweh, God of the Old Testament, it is not sufficient to show the apostle speaking of Christ in the same terms the ancient scriptures had used of Jahweh, nor that he replaced the person of Jahweh with the person of Christ when he quoted from the Old Testament. We must make an effort to enter into the spirit of the earliest Christian thought, for what Paul does is to take up its great themes. To do so, we must begin with the *facts* which were the starting-point of this thought. The essential fact is that of the Resurrection : on that day the prophecy of Psalm 110 reached fulfilment, the prophecy which Christ himself had quoted in reference to himself : 'You will see the Son of Man sitting at the right hand of Power'. Those divinely inspired words of Psalm 110 are addressed to the Messiah-King and imply the divinity of the Messiah, and this was made perfectly clear in the dispute Jesus had with the Jews over this text.

Besides this basic event, there are a number of others, in which the first Christians realized that Christ was taking the place of the God of the Old Testament, of Jahweh : it was through calling on the Name of Jesus that salvation was henceforth offered to those who believed, as the cure of the lame man showed; it was Christ seated at the right hand of God who sends the Spirit; it was Christ who was resplendent with the glory which until now had been the prerogative of Jahweh, God of the Old Testament; and it is Christ who will come again at the end of time to pass judgement on living and dead, a function formerly proclaimed as Jahweh's. With that in mind, they could rightly understand how Jesus of Nazareth, the Christ, could claim in the fullness of its meaning the transcendent Name, the Name of Jahweh. He is in truth the Lord, and all creation can and *must* bend the knee to him in token of their adoration : 'God has highly exalted him and bestowed on him the name which is above every name, that at the name of Jesus every knee should bow, in heaven and on earth and under the earth, and every tongue confess that Jesus Christ is *Lord,* in the glory of God the Father' (Phil. 2 : 9-10).

B. Before the Incarnation

God from eternity

We have seen the importance of the resurrection in the early Christian's realization of the divinity of Christ. Paul even speaks of it in a way which may cause some difficulty : 'Christ was *constituted* Son of God, in power . . . as a result of the resurrection' (Rom. 1 : 4); on the day of his resurrection the words of Psalm 2 reached fulfilment : 'You are my Son, today I have begotten you'; Christ received the Name above every name on the day of his exaltation. We might justly ask whether Paul thinks that Christ only became Son of God, really God, on the day of his resurrection. Was Christ no more than a man, and did he only receive a divine character and divine prerogatives when the power of God raised him from the dead and raised him to his right hand 'in the heavenly places' (Eph. 1 : 19-20)? The answer is no. Although these expressions may suggest the opposite (and we will account for them in due course) Paul believed in the pre-existence of Christ, in his pre-existence as Son of God, and as God.

The name *Kyrios* implies, as we have seen, Christ's dominion over the whole world, heaven as well as earth. More precisely, the Messiah-King in the prophecies of Psalms 110 and 2 overcomes one by one all his enemies, all the Gentiles who had rebelled against God, and brings them back to subjection. In the prophecies of the second Isaiah, however, Jahweh is also depicted as the conqueror of the Gentiles.

8

He holds them all in his power and does with them as he
wills; and this dominion is based on *his creative power;* it is
because he is the creator of the universe that Jahweh is its
King, its absolute master.

> Jahweh sits above the boundaries of the earth,
> And its inhabitants are like ants;
> He stretches out the heavens like a curtain
> Drapes them like a tent to dwell in;
> He brings princes to their knees,
> And makes the rulers of the earth nothing. . . .
> To whom then will you compare me
> That I should be like him? says the Holy One.
> Lift up your eyes on high and see :
> Who created these stars?
> He who brings out their host one by one,
> Knows them all by name;
> By the greatness of his might,
> And because he is strong in power
> Not one is missing (Is. 40 : 22-26).

The same ideas can be found set out in Isaiah chapter 45 :
God is creator of heaven and earth (vv. 18-19), which is the
reason why all nations will come offering their homage and
will destroy their useless idols (vv. 20-22), while every knee
will be bent before Jahweh and every tongue will profess
that he is the only God (vv. 23-24). (This passage will be
recognized as the one quoted by Paul at the end of his christological hymn in Philippians.)

Consequently if Jahweh is worshipped as master of the
whole world and of all nations, it is because he is creator of
the universe. And the same is true of Christ : he was enthroned as King-Messiah on the day of his resurrection, because in actual fact the whole universe was created through

him. Paul, in 1 Corinthians, explicitly draws a connexion between the title of Lord and the creative power of Christ. After a solemn statement of the unity of God, which he contrasts with the numerous idols of pagans, he goes on : 'Yet for us there is one God, the Father, from whom are all things and for whom we exist; and one Lord, Jesus Christ, through whom are all things and through whom we exist' (1 Cor. 8 : 16). The Father is the origin and end of all things, the Lord is the one through whom all things were made. Paul develops this idea in the letter to the Colossians :

> God (the Father) has delivered us from the dominion of darkness and transferred us to the kingdom of his beloved Son. . . . He is the image of the invisible God, the first born of all creation : for in him all things were created, in heaven and on earth, whether thrones or dominions or principalities or authorities—all things were created through him and for him. He is before all things and in him all things hold together (1 : 13-17).

This statement of Paul's can only be understood fully in the context of the current of thought from which it springs. The Christians at Colossae had allowed themselves to be affected by heterodox teachings, speculations about cosmic Powers (a foretaste of second century Gnosticism). One of their errors was to make Christ one of these other-worldly Powers, and the purpose of their controversy was to discover his precise dignity among the Powers. Paul stated vehemently that Christ was transcendent, and so cut short dangerous conjectures. Christ, he said, can in no way be compared with those heavenly Powers; he is greater than they and is their master; he belongs to an order of being different altogether from theirs. And the reason for this is that all things in heaven and on earth were created by him, in him and for

him. Nothing can exist apart from Christ, including those
heavenly Powers about whom the Christians at Colossae
were speculating. In his desire to assert Christ's complete
superiority over all the orders of heaven, Paul is led to state
specifically his transcendent origin : Christ, he says, transcends the created order, for that order was his own creation
—'he exists before all things'—a statement which implies a
temporal, but also a more important ontological priority.
The whole world belongs to the created order, but Christ is
no 'creature', he was 'begotten before every creature'.[15] He
is the uncreated Son through whom all creation came to be.

Paul goes on to make this more precise : 'He is the image
of the invisible God'. This phrase does not of itself necessarily
suggest the divinity of Christ; the author has already stated
in an allusion to Genesis 1 :27-28, that *man* is the image and
the glory of God (1 Cor. 11 :7). Nevertheless Paul draws a
very clear distinction between the situation of Adam and
that of Christ 'the second Adam'; still referring to Genesis,
he contrasts the first Adam who was 'of earth' with the second
Man, Christ, who was 'of heaven' (1 Cor. 15 :48). We may
ask whether Christ would be 'the image of God' because he
is 'of heaven', in virtue of his transcendent origin as Son of
God. This has often been accepted, but the passage of
Corinthians does not seem able to bear that interpretation.
Paul's thought is conditioned by the resurrection, and in
saying 'the second man is of heaven', he is thinking less of
the Son's transcendent origin than of Christ's present state in

---

[15]The phrase in Colossians 'first born of every creature' must
also be understood in this way. Paul repeats time and time again the
truth that *everything* was created through Christ; therefore he cannot be saying that Christ is the first of creatures. The genitive
pasès ktiseôs in this phrase must be a genitive of comparison,
implicitly governed by the word *protos* (first) in *Prôtotokos* (first-
born), and this word 'first' must then have a temporal sense,
'before'.

glory with his human body. This interpretation is clearly supported by similar passages in Philippians and Colossians.[16] Other texts where Christ is called the 'image of God' in virtue of the glory he has received by the resurrection must also be interpreted in the sense we have suggested.[17]

But the context of the letter to Colossians is different. Paul is not discussing, at least in the extract which concerns us, the glory of risen man. To understand his thought here, we must consult the sapiental writings of the Old Testament, by which Paul was obviously influenced. In the Book of Proverbs, Wisdom sings in praise of herself; her origin was 'from the beginning, before the earth was made'; she was not herself created but was brought forth, the first to appear before all things on earth; and she took part in the work of creation (Prov. 8 : 22-30). We find here the main ideas which Paul has applied to Christ in Colossians. Wisdom is pictured, in another place, as 'breath of the power of God, pure efflu-ence of his glory who is the all-powerful God; she the un-tarnished mirror of God's majesty; she, the faithful image of his goodness' (Wis. 7 :25-26). Surely Christ then is 'the image of the invisible God' even as divine Wisdom was 'the reflection of God's glory, its effluence, its mirror'. The writer of Hebrews projects us into the same current of thought when he speaks of the Son : 'Whom God appointed the heir of all things, through whom also he created the world. He reflects the glory of God and bears the very stamp of his nature, upholding the universe by his work of power' (Heb. 1 : 2-3). Christ is, therefore, 'the image of the invisible God', even as the Wisdom of God is, not only by reason of the glory which took possession of him on the day of his resurrection, but also because he is the Son, begotten of the Father before time began. The earliest Christians and Paul were greatly

[16]Phil. 3:20-21 and Col. 3:1-4.
[17]2 Cor. 3:18 and 4:4-6.

helped to this understanding of Christ's pre-existence as God by Jewish speculation on the nature of Wisdom, which tended to make Wisdom a full person, distinct from God.

The One who is sent

Here again the writings of the Old Testament had carved the way in preparation for an identification of Jesus of Nazareth and the Wisdom of God. God, it had been said, would send Wisdom to earth one day in order to bring help to, and bestow heavenly gifts upon mankind. In the same way it was foretold that the Word of God, which for all practical purposes was regarded in Jewish thought as identical with Wisdom, would be sent on to the earth. And time and again Christ had reiterated to the disciples that he had been sent by his Father. Paul, therefore, does no more than repeat this idea when in the letter to Romans he asserts : 'God has done what the law, weakened by the flesh, could not do; sending his only Son in the likeness of sinful flesh' (Rom. 8 : 3). To the Galatians, he expresses it even better : 'But when the time had fully come, God sent forth his Son, born of woman, born under the law, to redeem those who were under the law, so that we might receive adoption as sons' (Gal. 4 : 4). God was to send his Wisdom, his Word, begotten before time began; God did send his Son, the Wisdom of God, the Son who pre-existed in God before ever any creature was made in heaven or on earth.

It is clear then that this Son, begotten by God before all ages, can be no other than God himself. St Paul asserts this forcibly in the hymn in Philippians. Christ was 'of divine condition'; or, to use a phrase closer to the Greek, he was 'in the form of God' : but he emptied himself, taking the form of a slave, becoming like men, refusing to cling to that 'equality with God' which he could have claimed. 'Outside his humanity Christ has no other state of being than a divine state of being. He has his being in God; this means that he has a state of being like God, equal to God; consequently he has a strict right, a natural right to the privileges of God— majesty, glory, power over the universe. His humility consists in the fact that he refused to acquire these privileges other than by the way of submission and obedience.'[18]

The Trinity

The belief in Christ, Son of God, really divine, finds its most perfect expression in the formulas in which the Lord Christ appears, together with the Holy Spirit, as of equal standing with God the Father. Christ and the Holy Spirit are distinguished from God because they are named separately from him. Paul, however, expressly puts them side by side in closely balanced formulas to show clearly that God, the Lord, and the Spirit are members of one and the same divine order of being. He writes to the Ephesians : 'There is one body and *one Spirit*. . . . *One Lord,* one faith, one baptism; *one God and Father* of us all' (Eph. 4 : 4-6).

Similarly, in his first letter to the Corinthians, he wants to show that the church is one in spite of the diversity of charismatic gifts; and he does so thus :

There are varieties of gifts, but the *same Spirit;*
there are varieties of service, but the *same Lord;*
there are varieties of working, but it is the *same
God* who inspires them in every way (1 Cor. 12 : 4-6).

He ends his second letter to Corinth with this epitome :

'The grace of the *Lord Jesus Christ* and the love of *God* (the Father) and the fellowship of the *Holy Spirit* be with you all' (2 Cor. 13 : 14).

[18]Cerfaux, op. cit., p. 291.

The Submission of the Son

It would be quite impossible to doubt that Paul regarded Christ as God, and as God from eternity. But it is still true that Paul's theology has not yet reached the perfection of John's, at least in its expression. His formulas are less clear, less precise, less detached from human ideas. There are many reasons for this.

In the first place, we must never forget that Christ's human nature did not dwindle and fade from view as Christians became more clearly aware of his divinity. Christ remains at once God and man, really God and, equally, really man. On the other hand, the apostles and disciples always remained under the vivid impression of what they first saw and knew of Christ. They knew him as a man who already gave them an inkling of an unearthly nobility but who was no less a man for all that. He ate and drank with them; he was prone to fatigue of body and disappointment of heart. When they spoke of him, they did not bother to distinguish, as we must, between Christ the God and Christ the man. Christ, the Son of God, the Lord, was always to them simply Jesus of Nazareth who had lived among them, who had humbled himself in order to be seen on earth as a man 'in the state of a servant'. Paul is no exception to this rule; and this accounts for those expressions which seem to reduce Christ to the status of a creature pure and simple. For example, it is God (the Father) who raised Christ from the dead; God is the God of our Lord Jesus Christ (Eph. 1 : 17); God is 'the head of Christ' as Christ is 'the head of man' (1 Cor. 11 :3). And in the same way that Jesus himself could say that no one, not the angels, nor *even* the Son, knew the hour of judgement, so Paul could say that at the end of time, 'when God has subjected everything to the Son, then even the Son will make submission to him who submitted all to him, that God may be all in all' (1 Cor. 15 :28).

Moreover, we know the important part played by the resurrection in this matter. But the resurrection affected Christ essentially in his humanity; and this then was another factor which led to the point of view that Christ was 'constituted', established, as 'Lord' from the moment of his resurrection. And again, the title 'Lord', as we have seen, implied essentially the idea of dominion over the world, over all hostile powers. In actual fact, however, Christ did not begin to rule, to exercise dominion, except as a result of his resurrection, and this is why the summaries which describe his exaltation give so much importance to the resurrection. Hence in the letter to the Romans, the phrase 'he was designated Son of God . . . as a result of his resurrection' must be understood in the light of this. Paul never makes any conjectures about the mystery of the Incarnation, the mystery of two natures united in the unity of a divine person. His chief consideration is the fulfilment of Psalm 2, the greatest messianic psalm of them all: 'You are my Son, today I have begotten you': and this whole psalm is concerned with the enthronement of the Messiah-King and his dominion over the nations who had revolted against God.

Paul, therefore, believed in the divine nature of Christ, in spite of the ambiguity of some of his expressions, which must not be interpreted too ingenuously. He professed that Christ pre-existed close to God, 'in the form of God'; begotten before time itself. He did not invent his belief in Christ's divinity under the influence of pagan religion. He discovered it in Christ's own words, experienced it on the Damascus road, and finally learned it from the tradition handed on to him by the earliest Christians.

The Divinity of Christ in Saint John

D. Mollat, S.J.

V

The Divinity of Christ in Saint John

D. Mollat, S.J.

THE WORD WHICH in John's writings most closely approximates to our abstract noun 'divinity' is that of 'glory'. It is admittedly a much less precise word, but it possesses an infinitely greater range of highly concrete overtones. It derives from the Old Testament, where the 'glory of God' described the terrifying brightness and overpowering intensity of the divine Presence. It was God himself, revealing himself in all the majesty and all the power that is his.

The New Testament applied this to Christ. The synoptic gospels, however, nearly always reserve it to the Son of Man coming on the clouds of heaven at the Parousia, in the splendour of his power. Luke alone applies it on two occasions to Jesus during his earthly life, once when the glory of God was seen surrounding the Messiah's cradle on Christmas night, and again at the transfiguration, when Christ appeared in overwhelming glory; but even this must be regarded as a kind of prophecy in action of the resurrection. John, on the other hand, ascribes glory to the Jesus 'dwelling among us' as a habitual characteristic; John had 'seen' his glory and gives testimony of it (1 : 14);[1] glory was evident in Jesus' miracles, which were like signs 'manifesting' it and revealing the supreme power bestowed on him by the Father and indicating that God was present and acting in him (2 : 11). But, for John, glory shone out most clearly at the passion, his 'hour' properly so called, the hour of the 'exaltation' and 'glorification' of the Son of Man (12 : 33-34). This exaltation

[1] All references are to the fourth gospel unless otherwise stated.

was itself the sign of the invisible glorification wrought in
Christ by his resurrection, by which he was finally re-
endowed with the glory he possessed with the Father before
the creation of the world (17:5). Yet that was not the end
of the matter, for Jesus wanted his friends to be associated
with him in his glory, and from that moment he communicated a share of it to them: 'The glory you have given me, I
have given to them that they may be one even as we are one'
(17:22). The principle of unity among the disciples was the
glory of Christ shining over them. Jesus was 'glorified in
them'. Eventually they would behold his glory in all its splendour. 'Father, I desire that they also, whom you have given
me, may be with me where I am, to behold my glory which
you have given me in your love for me before the foundation
of the world' (17:24).

Any study of Christ's divinity in John turns upon an
understanding of what the evangelist meant by this concept
of Jesus' glory. Such an understanding will clearly not be
derived in sufficient detail merely from a study of the word
'glory' alone. So we must try to examine the mystery of Jesus'
personality as John portrays it, and the formulas like
Messenger, Son of Man, Son of God, and Word, by which
he expressed it. The word 'glory' is really in the nature of a
synthesis of all these other expressions. We may merely note
that when John uses this word of Christ on earth—the word
which the synoptists reserve for the eschatological glorification of the Son of Man—this is already an indication that for
John 'the glory' belongs to the very being of Jesus, belongs to
that in him which is hidden from sight and is revealed only to
faith. We may also note the astonishing new departure in
applying to a man a word which formerly described God
himself revealing himself in power. No name like this had
ever before been bestowed upon prophet, king, priest or any
other man in the Bible. Never before had a sentence even

remotely resembling the following been written about a man : 'He manifested his glory, and his disciples believed in him' (2 : 11). For glory in the Bible belonged to descriptions of the appearances of God. By applying it to Jesus only one thing could be meant : that God had appeared on earth and had been revealed in all his power in Jesus. John actually underlines the essential sameness of the glory of God and the glory of Jesus : 'In him (the Son of Man) God is glorified' (13 : 31); 'If you believe, you will see the glory of God' (11 : 40).

It remains for us to specify the nature of the bond which binds these two 'glories' into one. John tells us what it was in his prologue : it is the bond between Father and Son; Jesus' glory was 'glory as of the only Son from the Father, full of grace and truth' (1 : 14). From the very beginning, then, this word glory tells us that for John the gospel is the account of a theophany, where fire, thunder, and lightning have given place to the appearance of a son of man, Jesus, who called God his Father.

A. The Dimensions of Jesus' Personality

The Fulfilment of Scripture

In John, Jesus appears as the focal point and culmination of the Scriptures. That is how Philip introduced him to Nathanael : 'We have found him of whom Moses in the law and also the prophets wrote, Jesus of Nazareth, the son of Joseph' (1 :45). Jesus applied to himself, in the conversations he had with the religious leaders of Judaism, these words : 'You search the scriptures because you think that in them you have eternal life; but it is they that bear witness to me . . . if you believed Moses, you would believe me, for he wrote of me' (5 :39, 46).

The witness of the Scriptures, for John, does not mean
only the prophetic references to things fulfilled by Jesus—to
his messianic entry into Jerusalem (12 : 4 ff) for example, or
to details of his passion (16 : 32; 19 : 24, 28, 36, 37), or to his
resurrection (20 : 9); it means also—and much more
fundamentally—the prophetic figures of Christ with which
the Bible abounds. It means that the whole history of
Israel is completely directed to Jesus, that it has
no meaning, no cohesion, no value except in him and
through him.

John does not deal with this history in a connected and
scientific way, but by allusions, in connexion with the liturgical feasts, and in the course of Jesus' discussions with the
Jews. But one after the other all the important moments of
that history are brought up. First of all, the history of the
Patriarchs. The story of Abraham appears in chapter eight,
in a discussion about Abraham's true sons. Jesus shows the
Jewish leaders that they are sons of the devil, murderer and
liar; he is 'the Son' foreseen by the Patriarch; it was of him
that the birth of Isaac gave promise and joyful hope : 'Your
father, Abraham, rejoiced that he was to see my day; he saw
it and was glad' (8 : 56). Isaac is perhaps referred to in the
interview with Nicodemus : 'For God so loved the world that
he gave his only Son' (3 : 16). The phrase is reminiscent of
God's instruction to Abraham : 'Take your son, your only
son Isaac, whom you love . . . offer him as a burnt offering
upon one of the mountains of which I shall tell you' (Gen.
22 : 2). And now Jesus is the only Son, whose sacrifice God
desired and whom he himself was to give for the salvation of
the world.

Jacob's story is suggested in two places. The first is in the
call of Nathanael. Nathanael was astonished at Christ's
supernatural knowledge; and Jesus replied : 'You shall see

greater things than these. Truly, truly I say to you, you will
see heaven opened and the angels of God ascending and
descending upon the Son of Man' (1 :50-51). This is an
evident allusion to Jacob's dream, wherein the patriarch had
seen heaven joined to earth, while the angels of God
ascended and descended a stairway. This dream was completely realized in Jesus, and Nathanael 'the true son of
Israel' (1 :47), would see with his own eyes what his fore-
father had seen only in dream and symbol : heaven opened
and truly united to earth in the person of Jesus. The second
reference to Jacob occurs in the incident with the Samaritan
woman. Jesus, who was sitting near the well given by Jacob
to his son Joseph, promised to give the woman a fountain of
living water. Her retort was : 'Are you then greater than our
father Jacob who gave us the well?' (4 : 12).

Moses is given much greater prominence in the fourth
gospel—so much indeed that it has been argued that the
whole gospel centres round him. His name occurs more frequently than any other. But the revelation given through
him is directed to and subordinate to God's revelation in his
only Son; the Law is subordinate to the gift of grace in Jesus
Christ; the covenant of Sinai is subordinate to the Incarnation (1 : 17). Christ was the one whom the Mosaic scriptures
had in mind, and so Moses will be the one to point
an accusing finger at the sceptics who would not understand him. 'It is Moses who accuses, on whom you set your
hope' (5 :45).

The main events of the Exodus are referred to Jesus. Christ
on the cross is compared to the bronze serpent raised up by
Moses to heal the Hebrews bitten by serpents (3 : 14). The
miraculous gift of manna had saved the Hebrews from
starvation, and the psalms and wisdom books had extolled
the marvellous qualities of this bread from heaven, this food
of angels; now Jesus himself interprets this passage in Exodus

9

and shows its real meaning : 'It was not Moses who gave you the bread from heaven; my Father gives you the true bread from heaven. For the bread of God is that which comes down from heaven and gives life to the world' (6 : 32-33). The manna of Moses' time was only a symbol of Jesus' descent from heaven in the Incarnation.

God ordered Moses to strike the rock, and water gushed forth to quench the people's thirst. Each year the Jews recalled this marvel in the liturgy of the feast of Tabernacles. And it was during the celebration of this liturgy that Jesus stood up in the Temple and proclaimed in a loud voice : 'if anyone thirst, let him come to me and let him who believes in me, drink' (7 : 37-38). Moses' rock was only the prophetic symbol of Jesus himself, and the water was symbolic of the Holy Spirit poured out by him abundantly upon the faithful.

As the Hebrews straggled across the desert, a pillar of fire went before them. In his comment on this phenomenon, the author of the book of Wisdom sees in it a symbol of the 'inextinguishable light' of the Law spread across the world by the holy people of God. Jesus referred it to himself. He announced that he was 'the light of the world' (8 : 12). In itself the image symbolized messianic salvation and everlasting life, but Jesus added : 'He who follows me will not walk in darkness, but will have the light of life.' The light going on ahead like a guide recalls the pillar of fire. Jesus is the guide who leads the people of God to life. The Bible, again, had frequently compared the chosen people to a flock of sheep led by their shepherd. The metaphor had been used to describe the Exodus, and this allusion is a vital element in the theme of the good shepherd. Moses, Aaron, and many others after them gave no more than an indication of the nature of the true shepherd of God's flock, Jesus Christ. An entire bliblical theme therefore is given its true meaning in Jesus (10 : 1-16).

The same is true of the figure of the vine. This was one of the images the prophets used to describe the relationship between Israel and her God, and it usually carried overtones of sadness expressing the disappointment felt by God at the bitter fruit produced by his chosen vine. Psalm 80 joined this image to its recollections of the Exodus, and Jesus took it up in his turn to assert : 'I am the true vine ... you are the branches. He who lives in me and I in him, he it is that bears much fruit' (15 : 1-8). Jesus is the vine who will not disappoint God's hopes. In him human kind will bear the fruit God had so long awaited from his people and had so long been denied.

There is, however, one image from Exodus which strikingly dominates the whole of the fourth gospel : the image of the paschal lamb. The lamb, which every Jewish family ate on the evening of the 14th Nisan, according to a time-honoured ritual, was an annual reminder of how Israel had escaped from the land that enslaved them, protected by the blood of the lamb from the sword of the avenging angel, and had undertaken their journey towards the Holy Land with their God as guide. Like the manna, like the water from the rock, and the vine, the cloud, the serpent, and the flock, this incident is given reference to Jesus. At the very beginning of the gospel, John the Baptist describes Jesus to his disciples as he approached in words pregnant with mystery : 'Behold the Lamb of God, who takes away the sin of the world' (1 : 29). Primarily, of course, his words recall the Servant of Jahweh who was loaded down with the sins of men and offered for them as a lamb of sacrifice. It is, however, clear that the evangelist's intention here was to harness together this image and that of the paschal lamb. We shall see later all the links which connect the Pasch with the passion of Christ.

Not only is the whole of the prophetic literature directed

towards Jesus, but in addition the prophets themselves seem
to retire into insignificance before him, as the patriarchs had
done. 'Abraham died, as did the prophets; and you say, "If
anyone keeps my word, he will never taste death". Are you
greater than our father Abraham who died? And the
prophets died! Who do you claim to be?' (8:52-53). The
question is answered by the evangelist when he recreates
what was perhaps the acme of prophetic vision, namely the
vision which Isaiah had of the glory of God in the Temple.
John refers this vision to Jesus: Isaiah, he says, 'saw his glory
and spoke of him (Jesus)' (12:41).

So then it was Jesus whose 'day' Abraham saw, who was
prefigured in Isaac, whom Jacob saw in a dream, whom
Moses proclaimed and whose glory scorched the eyes of
Isaiah. There is mystery in this man upon whom all the
history of his people focused and who illumined all with
his glory.

Yet there is more, for in a similar way Jewish worship
found its fulfilment in Jesus.[2] John's gospel is constructed
around the liturgical feats of the Jewish year, namely, three
Paschs, one unspecified feast, a feast of Tabernacles, and
one feast of Dedication. This is the setting in which are un-
folded those facts of Christ's life which John chose to preserve
from among a host of others. The solemn rites of the festivals
do not simply constitute an extrinsic framework for these
facts and for the discourses which comment on the facts; the
rites indicate and clarify the meaning and deeper significance of the events. Thus, the healing of the sick man at the
pool of Bethsaida derives its true importance from its connexion with the Sabbath, in that it becomes the sign of a
divine work greater than the Sabbath, the life-giving act of

[2]For a fuller explanation of these ideas see the introduction to
'L'Évangile selon saint Jean' in the *Bible de Jérusalem*, p. 32-36
(Paris, 1953).

the Son of God (5 : 1-18). Jesus' discourses on the rivers of living water (7 : 37-39) and on the joy of Abraham (8 : 56), as well as the healing of the man born blind at the pool of Siloam (9 : 1-41), can only be understood in relation to the festival of Tabernacles. The distinguishing features of this festival were the ritual of drawing water from the pool of Siloam and an exuberant joy connected with their messianic hopes. Jewish tradition drew a connexion between the joy of the feast and the joy of Abraham. Jesus placed himself firmly at the centre of this feast, because it was directed to him, it had no meaning except in him—he, the fount of living water, the joy of Abraham, and the light of the world.

John connects the feast of Dedication with the decision of a large number of the members of the Sanhedrin to have Jesus executed. The Dedication celebrated the liberation of the Temple and the nation by the Maccabees; and the Jewish leaders were afraid that the Romans, alerted by the messianic agitation inspired by Christ, might destroy the Temple and nation. 'It is expedient,' said Caiphas, 'that one man should die for the people, and that the whole nation should not perish' (11 : 49-50). John reveals a significance in this decision which the Jewish leaders never suspected; for Jesus' death would give to this feast of political and religious emancipation its real meaning. Jesus was really to win his people's freedom in a way the Maccabean heroes could not have done, because he 'would die for the nation, and not for the nation only, but to gather into one the children of God who are scattered abroad' (11 : 51-53).

But it is the feast of the Passover which has been brought into the closest relation of all to Jesus. At the very outset of his public ministry, Jesus first went up to Jerusalem to cleanse the Temple—the centre of the paschal liturgy—of the profanation which defiled it. This purification was symbolic of an even more radical reformation. He proclaimed :

'Destroy this temple and in three days I will raise it up'
(2 : 19), a statement which was in fact the proclamation of
his own destruction by Jewish hands, and of his resurrection
which would make his body the victim and the temple of the
new, genuine Pasch. Later, the multiplication of the loaves
is connected with the Pasch; even though it took place in
Galilee, far from the Temple, John points out that 'now the
Passover, the feast of the Jews, was at hand' (6 :4). This
comment gives the real meaning of the incident and of the
discourse on the bread of life; the flesh of Jesus, offered as a
sacrifice 'for the life of the world' (6 :51), is to be the food of
the new Pasch, the manna of the new Exodus. Finally, and
most important, the connecting of Jesus' death with the feast
of the Pasch allowed John to reveal its real meaning. He
dwells on this connexion with great insistence. He points out
that Jesus died on the evening of the 14th Nisan, in other
words, at the very hour when the paschal lamb was being
eaten in every Jewish household. He points out that sentence
was passed on Jesus at the sixth hour, at about noon, when
according to Jewish records everything leavened was removed from the house to be replaced by the azymes of the
Passover (19 : 13-16). Only after that did the feast begin in
earnest, and it seems to have been the evangelist's intention
to underline the coincidence. But John lays the greatest
stress on the action of the soldier who, instead of breaking his
legs, pierced Jesus' side (19 :31-37). He connects this with
the rubric of the paschal liturgy about the lamb : 'Not a bone
of him (it) must be broken'. For the beloved disciple, Christ
on the cross is the Paschal Lamb; and the Jewish Pasch was
itself only the prefiguring of the real Pasch, the redemption.
Christ's death is the true sacrifice, and in it all earlier worship is consummated.

Thus the gospel of John takes as its framework the solemn
liturgical feasts in order to point implicitly to Jesus as the

fulfilment of all ancient religion. Not only the history of the chosen people, but also the worship of Israel was brought to its close in the person of Christ. The Sabbath disappeared before him, the feasts reached perfection at his coming, and the Temple itself, the focus of the whole religion, gave way to the temple of his risen body, from which poured the fountain of living water to renew the world. Jesus revealed the religion 'of spirit and of truth' in its fullness. The whole of sacred history was the slow, step by step introduction to it. He adopted as his own, and disposed of as its lord, the entire religious inheritance of Israel, and he alone had the power to make it fruitful as God intended it should be.

The Saviour of the World

The terms of John's gospel, however, have a relevance and meaning which transcends the Jewish world and its religion. The appeal of Jesus is universal in its scope; it awakes an echo in every human heart. The benefits he offers, water, bread, light and so on, correspond to basic needs common to all men, and to satisfy them men had made gods for themselves. Jesus proffers his benefits to all without restriction. He is 'the light of the world' (8 : 12), bread for all, fountain open to all who thirst, the shepherd of all the children of God scattered throughout the world, 'the lamb who takes away the sins of the world'; he draws all men to himself, he is the answer to all those who are seeking the way towards the light. He is the truth, the life, the spiritual centre of the universe, 'the saviour of the world' (4 : 42). This new aspect of Christ's personality in the fourth gospel is the one we must now study.

The Truth

Jesus presents himself as the truth. He 'spoke the truth' (8 : 40, 45), he revealed the worship of God 'in spirit and in

truth' (4:23), he was the witness of truth and everything
about him rang true. He was 'the true light ... that was
coming into the world' (1:9), he gave the true bread, he
was the true vine, and he was sent by the one, true God. He
was the truth and 'every one who is of the truth hears his
voice' (18:37); the Spirit he bequeathed to his friends is 'the
Spirit of truth' (14:17; 15:26; 16:13).

This notion must not, however, be understood in a philosophical sense; it is religious in character. It means that in
Jesus Christ God reveals himself and gives himself really,
authentically and completely to man; he shows him how to
worship, he speaks to him, teaches him; gives him divine
food 'which continues to eternal life'; to his stumbling feet
he ensures true light; in his efforts to do good, he gives him
the certainty that 'his works are done in God'; he joins him
to the true vine and gives to his whole life the fruitfulness
and freedom of the sons of light. Man is 'consecrated in
truth' (17:19); he becomes truly holy and pleasing to God.
His religious aspirations, now limitless in their object, find
their true satisfaction.

The Life

The concept of life in John is close to that of truth; truth
is life and leads to life, as falsehood is death and leads to
death. Like his notion of truth, John's notion of life is religious; it has nothing in common with our modern biological
concept. It derives from the Old Testament and means first
and foremost man's eternal salvation, even as death signifies
its loss.

For the Old Testament, life was in the hand of God. God
gives life and God takes it away again; but more than that,
God is man's life. He supports the existence of his creatures,
gives them growth and brings them to completeness. Life is
given by the divine Word, by Wisdom, by the Law, by the

Scriptures; all of them issue from God and guide men to life. And in John's gospel, this divine privilege is in the hands of Jesus: 'For as the Father raises the dead and gives them life, so also the Son gives life to whom he will. . . . As the Father has life in himself, so he has granted the Son also to have life in himself' (5 : 21, 26). Jesus has replaced the Law and the Scriptures: 'You search the scriptures, because you think that in them you have eternal life . . . yet you refuse to come to me that you may have life' (5 : 39-40). His sayings are 'spirit and life', he has 'the words of eternal life' (6 : 63, 68); man's fate depends on this word. The man who listens to his word 'has eternal life' (5 : 24), the man who cherishes it 'will never see death' (8 : 51), his message is 'eternal life' (12 : 50). Jesus himself is 'the light of life' (8 : 12), he infuses into the believer's heart a fountain leaping up towards eternal life; he is the 'bread of life', the 'living bread . . . if anyone eats of this bread he will live for ever ' (6 : 48-51). He is the shepherd come to save the flock 'that they may have life and have it abundantly' (10 : 10). Life can only be obtained in him and by him: 'Unless you eat of the flesh of the Son of Man and drink his blood, you have no life in you' (6 : 53). Thus even as he is the truth, so is he the life: 'This is eternal life, that they know you, the only true God, and Jesus Christ whom you have sent' (17 : 3). 'He who believes in the Son has eternal life, he who does not obey the Son shall not see life' (3 : 36).

That Jesus and life are one entity was confirmed in that grand scale miracle, the raising of Lazarus from the dead. Jesus himself emphasized this significant fact: 'He said to her, "I am the resurrection and the life; he who believes in me, though he die, yet shall he live, and whoever lives and believes in me shall never die" ' (11 : 25-26).

That sentence contains one of the central themes of John's gospel. The apostle wrote it with a single aim: 'that believing

you may have life in his name' (20 : 31). And Jesus not only
promises this life, guarantees it and leads men to it; but he
gives it even now to those who believe in him. To have found
him is 'to have life' (5 : 46).

The Supreme Judge

With the notion of life is closely associated that of judgement; the two are intimately connected in biblical theology.
Jesus, who possessed dominion over life, was for John the
supreme judge precisely because power of life and death is a
sign of the highest judicial power : 'The Father . . . has given
all judgement to the Son' (5 : 22). John does not mention
the pomp and ceremony of judgement scenes such as the
synoptists describe; Christ for him is judge of the human
conscience simply by what he is. So truly were the light and
truth of God incarnate in him that his very presence is for
the world the judgement of God. The light which went out
from him was so pure and so discerning that the spiritual
calibre and real mettle of the human soul were laid bare before him. It uncovered the activities of the wicked, but for the
man who walked in truth 'it will be evident, when the day
comes, that his deeds were done in God'. None can escape this
judgement of Christ, to which the cross gives cosmic dimension; the death of Jesus is 'the judgement of the world' (12 :
31). The whole universe is confronted by the crucified Lord
on Calvary, and judged by him.

The Mystery

Such are the characteristics of John's view of Christ. He
is the consummation of his people's destiny; its history con-
verged on him and its religion reached perfection in him.
More than that, however, in him the fullness of divine truth
was offered to every man, divine life was given without

restriction, and the pitiless light which shone from him revealed the whole universe in its true colours.

What then is Jesus? John's gospel asks this question with more insistence than the other gospels, and delves perhaps more deeply into the mystery than any of the other New Testament writings. Nicodemus as the spokesman of the ruling class said to Jesus: 'Rabbi, we know that you are a teacher come from God; for no man could do these signs that you do, unless God is with him' (3:2); and the Samaritan woman, roused to curiosity by his answers, first asked him: 'Are you greater than our father Jacob?', then: 'Sir, I perceive that you are a prophet', and finally 'Can this be the Christ?' (4:12, 19, 29). The crowds said to each other in bewilderment: 'Yet we know where this man comes from' (7:27). Discussions with the Jewish leaders began to pin-point the problem more closely; the scene became dramatic: 'Who do you claim to be?' they asked. 'Are you greater than our Father Abraham?... Why do you keep us in suspense? If you are the Christ tell us openly' (8:53). They admitted to the man blind from birth that the mystery was beyond them: 'We do not know where he comes from' (9:29). The Greeks who came 'to see Jesus' seemed dumbfounded by the same enigma, and it intrigued Pilate too: 'Where are you from?' he asked, meaning not 'from what country?' but 'who are you, what is the mystery of your origin?' Even the pagan caught the suggestion of a more than human greatness.

B.   THE SON OF GOD

Foremost among the formulas which express John's answer to the problem raised in the previous section is that Jesus of Nazareth was 'the one sent', the one whom the Father consecrated and 'sent into the world' (10:36). To recognize him as such is the prerequisite for the possession of eternal life.

The expression is not in itself a statement of his divinity. It had already been used, for example, of the prophets, when God said to Jeremiah : 'I consecrated you : I appointed you a prophet. . . . To all those to whom I shall send you you shall go' (Jer. 1 : 5-6). John the Baptist was also described by St John as 'a man sent from God' (1 : 6). Yet there is a radical difference between Jesus and the prophets who had been sent by God. The latter were told of their mission on some particular day; until then they lived like other men; then suddenly the Word of God was made known to them by a sign, or in a vision, or by the dispatch of someone to inform them of their vocation. Moreover the Bible tells us of the shocked amazement with which they often greeted the revelation of God's call. Some tried to argue, and others bitterly bemoaned their lot. Human nature in Jeremiah, as in Moses, tried to release itself from the hand of God which burnt like fire. Nothing like that happened with Jesus. The coming down of the Spirit upon his head was not in order to make known to him his mission, but 'to manifest him to Israel', and to give John the Baptist the opportunity of testifying that he was 'the Chosen of God' (1 : 31,34). It was by his mission that Jesus seemed most aptly described, because his nature and his mission were the same. He once said to the apostles when they were urging him to eat a little food : 'I have food to eat of which you do not know. . . . My food is to do the will of him who sent me and to accomplish his work' (4 : 32-35). A modern scholar has put this point brilliantly in the words : 'Jesus did not only live for his mission, but he lived *on* it'.[3] The overriding difference between Jesus and the prophets was therefore this, that whereas the latter were

[3]R. Bultmann, *Das Evangelium des Johannes,* (Göttingen, 1941), p. 143 ff.

sent to convey a definite message or to carry out a well-
defined assignment, his mission—the very fact that he was
sent—constitutes his message and the work he had to do.[4] He
proclaimed his coming into this world as the object in which
men must believe in order to achieve salvation. He gave
thanks that his disciples believed that the Father had sent
him. The work of God which he had to do was simply his
coming into the world. The Jews asked him, as they would
ask an ordinary prophet, to teach them 'what must be done
to do the works of God'. Jesus replied : 'This is the work of
God, that you believe in him whom he has sent' (6 : 28-29).
The transition from plural to singular here is not without
significance; God did no action more fundamental than to
send Jesus into the world, and he who wishes to co-operate
in the divine plan need do nothing else than correspond with
the mission, the sending, by receiving him in faith. Jesus, of
course, 'was born and came into the world to bear witness to
the truth' (18 : 37) as he told Pilate—but to the pagan's sub-
sequent question : 'What is the truth ?' he replied : 'I am the
truth'. Jesus' mission as recorded in the gospel of John is
actually closer to the mission of the Word or of Wisdom in
the Old Testament than to that of the prophets, for like the
Word of Wisdom his mission is not subordinate to—is not

[4]Jean Guillet has recently put forward similar ideas with regard
to Jesus and the Holy Spirit: 'In Jesus the fullness of the Spirit
indwells....No prophet had ever possessed the Spirit to this
extent....The Spirit had come upon the Judges and Prophets as a
strange power from on high....They knew they were being held
spellbound by someone stronger than themselves and being led by
him wherever he wished them to go. Not so with Jesus in whom
there was never any suggestion of compulsion. He did not regard
the Spirit as an invader from outside, but freely held conversation
with him. Moreover, the Spirit was present at Jesus' bidding for he
had power over this all-mighty Power. He left his followers so that
he could bestow this Spirit upon them.' In *Lumen Vitae*, VIII, 1953,
pp. 28-30.

'lor'—anything else. The very presence of Jesus is the light
which illumines and saves the world.

There are many other similarities which connect Jesus'
mission with the mission of Wisdom. Jesus, like Wisdom or
the Law (which was its living expression), had a divine and
heavenly origin. He came from above, from heaven, from
God; he was close to God and 'came forth from him'. No
other prophet or messenger from God in the Bible was described like this. Jesus' mission is thus presented as a short
stay, a day of journeying or of work between a coming from
God and a return to him. His beginning and his end were
both deep in God: 'I came from the Father and have come
into the world; again I am leaving the world and going to
the Father' (16:28). His death carried him back to the
Father from whom he took his origin. He ascended to the
one who had sent him.

Like Wisdom, and in a sapiential style, Jesus invites men
to his banquet. He opened the fountain of life to them, he
was the light guiding them on the way to truth, and, like
Wisdom, he set up his dwelling in their midst. Yet while
Wisdom never became anything more than an imprecise
personification, Jesus himself was.a real man, whose life,
actions and conversation can be seen in the pellucid light of
history. A comparison with Wisdom or the Law or the Word
is not then enough to enable us to penetrate the mystery of
Jesus. Who is this one sent from heaven? The person of the
Son of Man takes us nearer to the secret.

Son of Man

Both John and the synoptists use the term Son of Man to
describe Christ. The implied transcendence which this
expression added to Jesus' messianic claim has already been
discussed in an earlier section, the implication being that this
Son of Man was the heavenly being of the apocalyptic writ-

ings who was endowed by God with the power of judgement and dominion. The expression retained its transcendent importance for John; it designates Jesus as the supreme judge whose summons would bring all men back from the grave on the day of the last judgement. But in John, more clearly even than in the synoptists, it expresses the heavenly origin of Jesus. The Son of Man was more than the figure of mystery 'who comes upon the clouds of heaven'; he was the one 'who descended from heaven' (3 : 13) to reveal 'the things of heaven' to men and to give them 'the true bread of heaven' (6 : 32). His heavenly origin serves as a guarantee for the divine and spiritual mysteries he reveals.

The title 'son of Man' in John, then, even more clearly than in the synoptists, endows Jesus' messianic actions with a heavenly, transcendent, mysterious and divine quality. It presents Jesus as the being come from on high, who was in the world without being of it, who descended from heaven and ascended there again, who belonged to heaven and not to earth. Moreover, he was the being who was 'in heaven' while he yet remained on earth, who was superior to all, and who bore within himself a mystery from the other world of which he was fully conscious but of which the world knew nothing : 'For I know whence I have come and where I am going, but you do not know whence I come or where I am going' (8 : 14). Above his head, heaven opened and the angels of God ascended and descended. Heaven and earth were united in him.

The fourth gospel does not just look forward, as the synoptists do, to the manifestation of this heavenly being in the distant future, coming on the clouds of heaven at the Parousia. John had already seen this manifestation on Calvary. He regards passion and glorification, 'raising up' and crucifixion, as one and the same action. He sees the cross upon which Christ was 'raised above the earth' as the symbol of his being raised up to heaven. The whole of his gospel seems to have been given direction by this vision of the Son of Man 'raised up'. We see it in his interview with Nicodemus; Jesus had to be 'raised up', in imitation of the bronze serpent, as the sign from heaven that salvation lay here. Later, Jesus pointed out to the Jewish leaders that they themselves would 'raise him up', in other words would crucify him, and would one day understand how it was that their own hands conspired to bring about his glorification, for in raising him up, they would be raising up the Son of Man and showing him dramatically to the world in the glory of his divinity. On the eve of his passion, Jesus at last spoke to the crowd of his 'raising up', and spoke of it as the hour of his glory and the hour of judgement upon the world. The crowd's only retort was: 'And who is this Son of Man?' (12:23, 31, 34). And so we come to the Passion, with its final vision of the crucified figure with the gaping side. There the theme of the Son of Man ends, with Zechariah's words; 'They shall look on him whom they have pierced' (19:37).[5] 'The cross which lifted Jesus above the earth ... revealed most strikingly that he really belonged to the domain of his heavenly Father. It manifested quite clearly that his real place was with God.'[6]

This revelation yet remained heavy with mystery. The crowd's question still awaited an answer: 'Who is this Son of Man?'

Son of God

Fr. Benoit's discussion of the synoptic gospels (pp. 59-92) has already pointed out that the title Son of God, as found

[5]Cf. Zechariah 12:10.

[6]A. Vergote, 'L'Exaltation du Christ en croix selon le quatrième évangile', in *Ephemerides Theologicae Lovanienses*, 1952, p. 13, 23.

in the Bible or in the extra-biblical thought of the first century, did not inevitably suggest sonship in the strict sense of
the word, that is, a sonship as the term of generative activity
by which a father's nature is transmitted to another. The title
often expressed no more than a special relationship between
a man and God in virtue of the mission with which the man
had been entrusted, or in virtue of the special love God manifested in his regard. Or in the religion of the Greek world it
could denote 'divine men'. In the fourth gospel itself, Jesus
reminds the Jews that in the scriptures God had said to some
men, princes or judges, 'you are gods' (10:34). As a result,
the title Son of God was sometimes in John's mind only a
kingly title referring to the Messiah. An example of this
usage is Nathanael's profession of faith : 'Rabbi, you are the
Son of God! You are the King of Israel!' (1:49) where the
juxtaposition of the title Son of God with that of the Davidic
Messiah makes this interpretation certain. A similar conclusion can be drawn from Martha's confession : 'I believe that
you are the Messiah, the Son of God, he who is coming into
the world' (11:27). Martha believed that Jesus was the long
awaited Messiah, which indeed is no more than the title in
itself implies. The formula 'Son of God' or simply 'the Son'
is in other places related closely to that of 'Son of Man', for
instance : 'The Son of Man must be lifted up, in order that
whoever believes in him may have eternal life. . . . For God
sent the Son into the world, not to condemn the world, but
that the world might be saved through him' (3:14-17). It
would, therefore, be reasonable to agree with Dupont that
in John 'the title Son of God is related on one side to the
title Messiah, and on the other to that of Son of Man'[7] and
that furthermore, it has a close connexion with Jesus' divine
mission.

[7] J. Dupont, *Essais sur la Christologie de saint Jean,* (Bruges
1951), p. 283-293.

This statement does not, however, exhaust all the significance of the title. The argument which begins to develop in chapter ten about the Son of God reveals that the Jews as well as Jesus regarded it in this instance not only as a messianic title, but also as an affirmation of divine sonship in the strict sense of the word. Jesus was accused of blasphemy because he called himself by this title. The Jews claimed his death for that same reason : 'We have a law, and by that law he ought to die, because he has made himself the Son of God' (19 : 7). A claim to be Messiah and no more was not of itself blasphemous and was not punishable by death. So it is certain that the title here expresses something truly divine and transcendent.

This is confirmed by the nature of the relations between Jesus and the one of whom he claimed to be the Son, by the way he speaks of his Father. Jesus was 'the only Son' given to the world by God as a living proof of his love. The term 'only Son' is not found in the New Testament outside the fourth gospel and derives from the Old Testament, where it was used to describe a deeply loved child. John in the prologue adds to the connotation of affection it possesses the idea of a unique kind of sonship. Jesus was the Only-begotten, the recipient of unparalleled glory from the Father, alone able to reveal the mystery of God. When he gave others 'power to become the children of God' (1 : 12), they are by no means described in the same terms as the one 'who was born, not of blood nor of the will of the flesh nor of the will of man, but of God' (1 : 13)[8]. Jesus was *the* Son'; God is his Father by a unique title, so that he is always called 'my Father', 'the

[8] 1:12-13—the reading adopted by the author is that used by the *Bible de Jérusalem* as nearest to the original. It contains at once, it will be observed, a reference to the eternal generation of the Son and also to the Virgin Birth of Christ. Cf. Lk. 1:26-38. This reading is not as far as I know adopted by any modern English translation. *Translator's note.*

Father' or just 'Father', and where necessary 'my Father and your Father' (20 : 17), never 'our Father'. He puts himself on a different footing from other men. The Temple is his Father's house. Jesus proclaimed his mission in his Father's name; he related what he had seen with the Father, who had given him to the world as the true heavenly bread. His Father glorifies him. In the Son's hands lay the disposal of the many dwellings within the Father's house. A bond of unequalled intimacy linked Jesus and the Father, a bond of mutual love, of knowledge, of joint activity, and of mutual sharing in the possession of all good : 'The Son can do nothing of his own accord, but only what he sees the Father doing; for whatever he does, that the Son does likewise. For the Father loves the Son and shows him all that he himself is doing' (5 : 19-20). 'The Father knows me and I know the Father' (10 : 15). 'All that is mine is yours, and all that is yours is mine' (17 : 10). They possess the oneness of mutual presence, of mutual indwelling : 'The Father is in me and I am in the Father' (10 : 38). Vision of one inevitably entails vision of both; to see Jesus is to see his Father (14 : 9), and they are both the object of a single act of faith : 'He who believes in me believes not in me but in him who sent me . . . the Father and I are one' (12 : 44; 10 : 30). As one scholar has remarked, the 'we' in this phrase is in itself an unprecedented claim,[9] which is matched by an astonishing promise : 'If a man loves me . . . my Father will love him, and we will come to him and make our home with him' (14 : 23). An attempt has been made to explain away these statements as formularies taken from Greek mystical thought, and to regard them simply as declarations made by Christ about his mission. But we must say here about the Son what we said earlier about the Envoy : his message and work are inseparable from his being. Jesus'

[9]F. Godet, *Commentaire sur l'Evangile de saint Jean*, (Paris, 1902), ad. loc.

message lay first and foremost in the revelation of what he
was, the Son of God, and in the manifestation of 'the glory
as of the only Son from the Father' (1 : 14). It was in this
manifestation of the Son living in the bosom of the Father,
and of the loving intercourse which makes Father and Son
one in a union of transcendence, that the revelation of the
God 'whom no one has ever seen' (1 : 18) was accomplished;
then the nature of God as Father was made known in all its
wonder : 'I have made known to them your name, and I will
make it known' (17 :26).

Jesus' work can only be adequately appreciated in this perspective, for he was 'sent' for no other purpose than to give
men 'the power to become children of God' (1 : 12) through
belief in his name, that is, belief in himself, the Son. He came
on earth for no other reason than to allow men to share with
him the love with which the Father had loved the Son 'before the foundation of the world' (17 :24); 'that the love
with which you have loved me may be in them and I in them'
(17 :26). But, as a recent writer has expressed it : 'Christ was
able to give us the power to become children of God precisely
because he was the Begotten of God. . . . The function which
Christ fills originates from his nature, from his essence.'[10]
The nature of the Son of God is the keystone upon which the
whole building depends. As for Paul the building depended
on the glory of the Risen Lord, so for John it rests upon the
glory of the Only Son of God.

A modern critic can nevertheless claim that the description of Jesus as Son of God does not connote any metaphysical statement. The paradox of the Christian faith, he
claims, is that divine revelation is present in a man, in this
man Jesus; there is no real difference between him and other
men except that he is the 'Chosen One of God', 'the one who

---

[10]M. E. Boismard, *St John's Prologue*, (London, 1957), p. 94.

is sent', the revealer in whom God speaks to man, and only to this extent, the Son. 'Jesus', this author continues, 'as revealer of God, reveals nothing except that he is the revealer'[11] to whom faith must be given; he is the meeting place of God and man. But this extrinsic and nominalist explanation of Christ's nature and work does not correspond to the evidence of the gospel. The gospel did not, of course, define Christ's nature in the metaphysical language of later theology, any more than did the other writings of the New Testament. The title Son of God and the privileges which follow from it refer globally to the man Jesus, without any explicit distinction of natures in him; the bond uniting Jesus to the Father in a transcendent union is described (rather than defined) in terms of a relationship of love and mutual knowledge. But it would be quite arbitrary to deny this description the force of a real revelation about his being. There existed a unity between Jesus and the Father which was more than the moral union of an obedient servant or a perfect envoy. It was more than the perfect union between the one who sent and the one who perfectly interpreted the thought and perfectly executed the wishes of the one who sent him. The Jews might consider a claim of that kind as outrageously proud, but they would not consider it blasphemy. They sensed a great deal more in statements like : 'My Father is working still and I am working'; they realized that 'Jesus called God his Father', making himself 'equal with God' (5 : 17-18). When Christ announced his oneness with the Father, the Jews wanted to stone him : 'For no good work, but for blasphemy; because you being a man, make yourself God' (10 : 33).

[11]T. Bultmann, *Theologie des Neuen Testaments*, (Tübingen, 1951), p. 413.

Before the Incarnation

The assertion that Jesus is God is supported by the declaration that he pre-existed, a concept which is given clearer formulation in John's gospel than in any other of the New Testament writings. Like Wisdom, Jesus is regarded as pre-existing before his earthly, temporal life. Not all the texts which seem to refer to this are equally probative; for instance : 'Your Father Abraham rejoiced that he was to see my day; he saw and was glad' (8:56) and 'Isaiah said this because he saw his glory' (12:41); these do not necessarily prove Christ's pre-existence, because if Abraham saw his day, and Isaiah his glory, it was 'from a long way off', as an event foreseen. The value of some of the passages in Jesus' priestly prayer is also questionable for this argument; for example : 'Father, glorify me in your own presence with the glory which I had with you before the world was made' (17:5) and also 'Father, I desire that they also . . . may behold my glory which you gave me in your love for me before the foundation of the world' (17:24)—in both of which Jesus was evidently referring not so much to the glory he possessed when he pre-existed with the Father, but to the glory which the Father destined for the incarnate Word for all eternity.

The language used in chapter six, however, leaves no room at all for doubt : 'What if you see the Son of man ascending to where he was before?' (6:62). And this is reinforced by the solemn proclamation in chapter eight. Jesus leads up to it gradually. He begins by saying to the Jews : 'If anyone keeps my word, he shall not see death' (8:51): that is, he is master of life and death. At that, there was much shrugging of shoulders and a titter from the crowd : 'Are you greater than our father Abraham who died? And the prophets died! Who do you claim to be?' (8:53). Jesus replied that Abraham had seen his day. The Jews seized upon his reply and twisted it to make him imply that he had seen Abraham : 'You are not yet fifty years old and have you seen Abraham ?' Jesus answered their question without ambiguity : 'Truly, truly, I say to you, before Abraham was, I am' (8 : 57-58). In the original text, a forceful contrast had clearly been intended between 'was', the attribute of a creature of time, whose existence had a beginning, and 'I am' which described an existence transcending time and history, in other words a divine mode of being in the strict sense of the word. When Jesus told the disciples that they would see 'the Son of man ascending to where he had come from', he may only have been referring to a relative kind of pre-existence, like that of Wisdom, a pre-existence in relation to his present state. But in chapter eight he was laying claim to an absolute kind of existence, the existence possessed only by God. The divine nature of his claim becomes even more certain when we realize the connexion between his 'I am' and the 'I am' which is the divine name revealed to Moses and used by Isaiah. Jesus not only claimed a mode of existence proper to God, but also called himself by that name which summed up all the faith of Israel, and to which the whole history of Israel was intended to bear witness. The Jews made no mistake about it. They understood him so well that they picked up stones to kill him as a blasphemer.

A similar affirmation that Jesus possessed an absolute mode of existence is to be found in the words of John the Baptist : 'After me comes a man who ranks before me, for before me, he was' (1 : 30). The significance of these words is not adequately brought out in the way they are usually translated. 'The force of the assertion turns on the verb, which is relegated to the end of the clause ... John the Baptist declares : "Before me, he was"; as Christ will say later : "Before Abraham was, I am". The being of Christ is set in an absolute which transcends time."[12]

My Lord and my God

As we have seen, the Jews accused Jesus of 'making himself the equal of God' or more bluntly of 'making himself God' (5 : 18; 10 : 33). And 'Jesus is God' is the most certain and the most sacred truth in John's thought. Through the apostle Thomas, the gospel leads us to this explicit profession of faith : 'My Lord and my God!' (20 : 28), which recalls and develops that ancient Christian ejaculation 'Lord Jesus'—itself an expression of belief in his godhead.

The Word of God

In the prologue to his gospel, John has made a synthesis embracing all his christological reflection. We can find there most of the main lines of thought we have been considering, gathered together in a vision of tremendous scope which begins with eternity and embraces the whole history of revelation. John goes back to 'the beginning' (1 : 1), to the day of creation, when apart from God nothing existed. Yet in that mysterious, brooding 'beforehand', before any temporal existence, when imagination loses itself in the void, someone existed with God, someone distinct from the one here called God and yet himself God. This is not the blurred personification of Wisdom in the Old Testament, but the Word who exists with God, as one person with another, mysteriously united to God and sharing his eternal moment : 'He was'.

John then goes on to recall the highlights of the world's history in its relation to the Word. The Word, who was before all things, created all things, and nothing was brought into

[12]Boismard, *St John's Prologue*, op. cit., p. 59.

existence without his creative intervention. He is the principle of all being, the source of all life, and the light which
enlightens every man. But he did not remain remote, a
stranger to the world which is his work. He was in it, it was
his 'home', he 'comes' there. Finally, he himself takes part
in the history of the world. He became 'flesh', took on weak,
human nature, and made his home among us, making the
intense glory of the Word shine through human features.
And then a mysterious personality is revealed : he is 'the
Only Son'.

Then for the first time John mentions his human name :
'Jesus Christ', and compares it with the name of Moses, the
greatest of all the spokesmen through whom God had until
then announced his Wisdom to men. The contrast is vivid.
There are two mediators, two revelations, two covenants. On
one side a man, on the other the creative Word; on one side
the Law, on the other grace and truth; on one side something
given, on the other its fullness and fulfilment. John can then
conclude : 'No one has ever seen God; the only Son who
is in the bosom of the Father, he has made him known'
(1 : 1-18).

That is John's vision of Jesus : the eternal Word, God,
creator of the universe, the Son, only begotten of the Father,
who came on earth as a human being to make God known to
us and to make us his children. Nowhere else in the New
Testament, not even in the hymn to Christ in Colossians, is
there to be found such a magnificent expression of faith in
the divinity of Jesus. The origin and significance of this
theology of the Word is a matter for research, but it becomes
more and more accepted that it has close connexions with
the biblical theology of the Word of God, of Wisdom, and
of the Law—in other words, with the progressive history of
divine revelation which 'Jesus Christ the incarnate Word of

God sums up, recapitulates and fulfils'.[13] When he calls Christ the Word, John is attempting primarily to express his role as revealer, which since creation began is his role for the world and for men : he speaks God for them. But this does not mean that to give him the name 'Word' is purely functional, telling us nothing about the divine personality of him who bears it. This is to make a false distinction between Christ's mission and his being. Boismard says : 'His work is to reveal God to men, but this is itself founded upon the very nature of Christ; before all revelation he was already in a certain sense the Word of God, (just as the Sapiential books say of Wisdom that she was Wisdom in God even before the work of creation), he was in a certain sense the expression of the thought of God.'[14] This is the summit to which John leads us.

C. The Man Jesus

It remains to ask whether the divinity of Christ, so clearly stated in John, does not eclipse the historical reality? Can John's presentation of Jesus as a transcendent being, the claims to divinity he ascribes to him, and the supernatural bearing he attributes to him, can all these be given a historical basis? Is Jesus of Nazareth the same exalted Jesus who could read men's hearts, the master of history, he who demanded belief, who claimed to precede Abraham, and who made himself the equal of God? Would it not be more probable to suppose that this Jesus was actually a figment of John's mind, a kind of idealization of the real Jesus, and a Christ divinized by faith long after he had left the world? Loisy distinguishes different strata in the gospel, corresponding to different

[13]S. Lyonnet, 'Hellénisme et Christianisme', *Biblica,* XXII, (1945), p. 130.

[14]Boismard, *St John's Prologue,* op. cit., p. 94.

documents; and he claims that the author of the basic docu-
ment 'knew only a liturgical Christ, the object of Christian
worship'. No impression of reality is communicated by the
fragments of a divine biography he composed. Jesus is the
Saviour whom his followers worship when they celebrate his
mystery : 'The Christ of this gospel ... was not born of a
woman, as Paul's was, nor had he lived under the Law. He
is a form of god manifested in man ... a god who dies ...
and returns to life immortal to endow his followers with
immortality.'[15] Therefore, in Loisy's view, the author of
the fourth gospel has idealized the historical person Jesus and
transferred him to the ranks of the divinities in the mystery
religions. Some other writers consider that the idealization
was brought about through borrowing some of the characteristic ideas of Philo of Alexandria, and others again that it
owes much to Hermetic literature. For Albert Schweitzer,
Joannine theology is only the hellenization of Pauline
mysticism. And today, liberal critics no longer seek the
origins of John's christology in hellenistic syncretism, but
turn instead to oriental Gnosticism : St John made some
modifications to the person of the heavenly envoy in the
gnostic myth and applied it to Christ.

One after another, these hypotheses reveal their weakness.
It is not now possible to uphold seriously that there is any
link between the Christ of John and the gods of the mystery
religions. The dissimilarities between the *Logos* of John and
the *Logos* of Philo, between the historical symbolism of the
fourth gospel and the allegorical exegesis of the Alexandrian
thinker, are no longer arguable. While resemblances of language and imagery between John's gospel and pagan gnostic
writings cannot be denied, these do not establish a relationship of origin between them. The doctrinal content of the
fourth gospel is utterly different and always draws us back

[15] A. Loisy, *Le Quatrième Evangile,* (Paris, 1921), p. 56-58.

towards Jewish tradition. Any idealization of Jesus' personality that there is has taken place within the confines of this tradition, within the vision presented by biblical thought and the Christian faith.[16]

But the suggestion that the Jesus of history was transformed into a Jesus of faith can be seen to be baseless. We may notice first that John and the synoptic writers are agreed on one fundamental fact, the event towards which Jesus' whole life was directed. Both John and the synoptists are unanimous in affirming that Jesus was sentenced to death because he stated before the leaders of Judaism that he was the Messiah-Son of God. There is even a striking similarity between the Sanhedrin trial as recorded by Luke (perhaps the oldest form), and the alteration found in chapter ten of the fourth gospel. On both occasions Jesus was required to say whether he was the Christ, and on both occasions he was found guilty on the basis of a reply which was construed as a claim to be the Son of God in the transcendent meaning of the expression. In certain respects this episode is the pivot of John's gospel. Throughout the whole gospel, John is describing the trial of Jesus. Christ's testimony on his own behalf, supported by the Father's testimony to him, by his own 'works' and by the Scriptures, and finally confirmed by the Baptist's authority, is disputed step by step up to the final verdict of death; and the evangelist himself, enlightened by the witness of the Paraclete, intervenes in the case and adds his own evidence to declare that Jesus was truly the Son of God as he had claimed. There is a complete absence of mystical idealism in John. His desire was to bear witness, as one of the last and most qualified to do so, in the historical trial in which his Master's life was at stake. There

[16]A most valuable English account of the origins of the gospel is to be found in C. H. Dodd, *The Interpretation of the Fourth Gospel,* (Cambridge, 1954). *Translator's note.*

is a hint of this in the discourse after the Last Supper:
'You also (in union with the Spirit of truth) are witnesses, because you have been with me from the beginning'
(15:27).

His agreement with the synoptic writers is complete on
all essential points. All four equally take the sign from heaven
at the time of Jesus' baptism as their first point of reference.
They all recognize that Jesus worked a large number of
miracles. They all record his attitude of freedom from, and
his authority over, the Jewish rites of purification, the
Sabbath, the Temple, the Law and the Scriptures. They are
in agreement over his struggle with Satan and over the messianic mystery which enveloped his personality and so disconcerted the crowds. The most characteristic ideas of the
fourth gospel are already to be found in germ in the synoptists, where he was already described as 'the one sent', 'the
one who came', 'he who came forth'. John gives the title 'Son
of Man' a slightly different aspect, but the basic idea remains
the same, the transcendent, heavenly Messiah of the tradition derived from Daniel; and like the synoptics, John faith-
fully preserves the connexion which Jesus established
between the Son of Man and the passion. As for the title Son
of God, we have already seen that in the crucial episode of
the trial it has an identical significance both for the synoptists and for John. In the synoptists again, as in John, Jesus
never says 'Our Father'; he says either 'your Father' or,
much more often, 'my Father' (a dozen times in Matthew):
and this is a fact which has no real parallel in Jewish or Christian literature of that time. The text of Matt. 11:25-27 and
Luke 10:21-22 has already been dealt with in pp. 77-78;
this text, certainly authentic, describes the relationship of
Christ to his Father in a manner so similar to that of John
that it has been described as a 'Joannine meteorite' fallen into
the synoptic texts. The awareness shown by Christ that he

possessed a relationship with God so deep and so intimate
that it set him apart from all men is thus affirmed in the
gospel tradition long before John.

It is certainly true that John's gospel represents a more
advanced stage of reflection on all the material it has in
common with its predecessors—the mission of Jesus, his
heavenly origin, his union with the Father, his pre-existence.
Nevertheless this cannot be called a creation; John is faithful
to the earliest Christian tradition. This is proved by the fact
that his work contains traces of a very primitive christology
—a sign that his witness is true. He never shrinks from using
the humblest titles to describe Christ : for example, Jesus was
not only the Word, he was also the one called Rabbi or Rab-
boni, Messiah, Son of God in the Davidic sense of 'king of
Israel'; he is called 'the chosen of God' (to adopt the reading
of many good manuscripts), and 'the prophet'. This latter
title incidentally was one of the first to be used in the christology of Acts, as an earlier essay has shown. Finally Jesus
was 'the Lord and the Master'. These titles, found side by
side with the most sublime declarations, bear the imprint of
reality; they give the lie to Loisy's statement quoted
earlier (p. 155) : 'The author knows only a liturgical Christ,
object of Christian worship'.

But John's whole portrait of Jesus gives an undeniable
impression of life and truth. The Word made flesh, while
possessing the supreme majesty of the Son, still remains Jesus
the man, who sat tired and thirsty by Jacob's well and begged
a little water, who wept at the tomb of Lazarus, who was
troubled even to anguish at the thought of his approaching
Hour and the treachery of one of his own friends. And Jesus
the man translated the most sublime things of God into the
simplest language, became his disciples' servant and washed
their feet, listened to the most childish questions from them
even when he was attempting to confide high and important

truths to them. Nothing could equal the familiarity and natural charm with which he greeted his followers after his resurrection, when one might have expected the impact of unbearable glory.

The gospel remains rooted in history, even while it stands as the acme of the earliest Christian reflection on Jesus' divinity. There is no fraud or deceitful fabrication here; on the contrary it remains at once the most profound and the most faithful record of what from the very beginning, in no matter what archaic forms of expression, Jesus had been for his own : the Son of God.

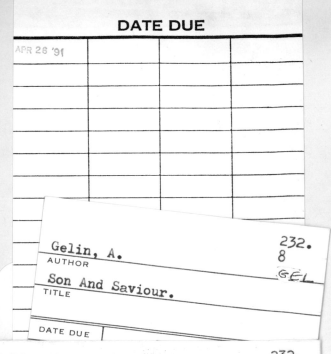

Gelin, A.

AUTHOR

Son And Saviour.

TITLE

DATE DUE

232.
8

GEL

Gelin, A.
Son And Saviour.

232.
8
GEL